What others are saying about this book

"As a faithful and avid reader of Linda Schurman's newsletters since their inception in 1990, I continue to be inspired and uplifted by her intuitive insights and powerful wisdom.

Linda is a gifted author who encourages people to improve the quality of their lives, while empowering all of us to be important contributors in creating a world that is cooperative and peaceful.

Linda writes from the heart with important messages worthwhile reading - I highly recommend her book to every-one!"

— S. Maria Giordano, MSW,LCSW

"What sets Linda Schurman's prognostications apart, aside from her uncanny accuracy, is her ability to provide a perspective in which to make sound decisions. This book should be the most dog-eared in your library as you return to its pages to garner understanding of the events unfolding around us, to decide how to face them, and maybe even to gather the courage to do something to help make the world a better place for all of us!"

— Kathleen Spiliotopoulos, Entrepreneur and Business Consultant.

D0896189

"When Linda Schurman speaks, I listen. Her insightful, accurate vision applies her vast experience with ancient wisdom and the research and scholarship of today's most respected thinkers. She looks at the confluence of cosmic and worldly trends and how this knowledge can be used to guide the creation of our individual lives and the social, political and economic future of our planet. Linda has counseled me for 30 years through the changes in my personal life with accuracy and caring. She sees the immense challenges, but also the immense possibilities for humans to transform our world and our destiny. And she offers factual information that can guide us to use astrological influences for the benefit of all rather than defaulting by our inaction."

— Arlene Muzyka, Art Therapist and Professional Musician

What Next?

A Survival Guide to the 21st Century

What Next?

A Survival Guide to the 21st Century

by

Linda Schurman

Lazer Lady
Publishing

What Next? A Survival Guide to the 21st Century

By Linda Schurman

Copyright © 2007 Linda Schurman

Published: June 2007

ISBN: 978-0-9796900-2-0

Published by

Lazer Lady Publishing, Inc.

2505 Anthem Village Dr., Ste. E-165

Henderson, NV 89052

www.lazerladypublishing.com

Edited by Linda Lane

Book design and layout by Tony Stubbs, *www.tjpublish.com*

Cover art by Shelley Szajner, *www.shelley-szajner.com*

Printed in the USA

Table of Contents

Dedication

To my grandchildren: Emily, James, C.J., Maria, Michelle, Rachel and Kiley – all of whom inspire me to care so passionately about the future.

Acknowledgements

I wish to thank Linda Lane, my editor and publisher, for giving me the opportunity and encouragement to write this book; for her patience, kindness and valued experience without which I could never have embarked upon this adventure.

I also wish to express my appreciation to my husband, Richard, and my mother, Margaret, for their continued support, and my son, John, for his help and assistance.

Introduction

A fascination with the art of prophecy has been with us throughout the ages and has been present in the records of every major civilization. Some of history's most famous soothsayers were The Oracle of Delphi of the ancient Greeks, the Biblical prophets of Jewish and Christian traditions, the predictions from the Hindu Puranas, the prophecies of the Hopi Indians, the Toltecs, Aztecs, and Mayans of Mesoamerica, the famous prophecies of Nostradamus, and modern day psychics such as Edgar Cayce, the so-called Sleeping Prophet.

Frequently, prophecies are framed within doom and gloom scenarios, trapped by a cascade of events perceived as "fate." In addition, the predictions are often shrouded in "code" or simply difficult to decipher, leaving us to line up actual events with what we think they originally meant. The "debunkers" have a good time throwing rocks at the validity of the original prophecies and their overall vagueness and inaccuracy. They have a point well taken. However, the real problem that presents itself is how to interpret a future for which we have no frame of reference. For example, how clearly could a seer like Nostradamus, whose experiences are defined by life in the 16th century, describe an airplane, a helicopter, a submarine or a skyscraper?

Translating the Constellations

A definition of astrology is: "The study of astronomical events in relationship to the occurrence of historic cycles and themes that are relevant to our lives."

The field of astrology itself is around 4,000 years old and holds the distinction of being an important and highly revered subject in all the world's major ancient societies. Arising historically at the time of the agricultural revolution, it became necessary, through the study of the perceived movement of the sun and the phases of the moon, to carefully time the coming and going of the seasons so farmers could plant and harvest their crops. As civilizations developed written languages, astronomical observations literally evolved into the creation of calendars. In the ancient world, astronomy and astrology were contained within one subject of study and they did not separate until around the time of the European Renaissance. Planetary movements were used to predict probable events such as famines or floods, wars (victory or defeat), and the futures of important rulers of the dominant empires of the times.

Historians believe astrology began in ancient Babylonia (modern-day Iraq) with the publication of their great astrological work *The Illumination of Bel*, compiled within the period 2100 – 1900 B.C. It was a respected subject of study in ancient Egypt, Persia, Greece, Rome, China, India, and the Maya and Aztec cultures of Central and South America. In the New

Testament of the Bible, the three wise men following the star to the birthplace of Jesus were said to be astrologers who predicted this monumental historic event. During what we call the "Dark Ages" in Europe, astrology flourished in the empires of what is now the Middle East when the Arab and Islamic nations were advancing in mathematics, astronomy, art and architecture. The famous physician and prophet Nostradamus studied and practiced astrology, which was part of most university curricula in 16th century Europe.

Some luminaries who have been students or practitioners of astrology through the ages are: Hippocrates, Claudius Ptolemy, Paracelsus, Tycho Brahe, Johannes Kepler, Sir Isaac Newton, Sir Francis Bacon, St. Thomas Aquinas, Benjamin Franklin, Ralph Waldo Emerson, U.S. President Theodore Roosevelt, and U.S. President Ronald Reagan, to name only a few.

Forecasting in the 20th and 21st Centuries

In more recent times, astrologers have had a great deal of success tracking financial markets, and frequently publish newsletters that are widely followed by investors. Millions of individuals make use of private readings by astrologers who offer them a deeper understanding of their personal journeys through life. A growing number of astrologers in our present era are captivated by the insights planetary patterns offer us with respect to the cycles of war, economic booms and busts, and the emergence of political and religious ideologies.

What mostly differentiates astrologers today from their ancient counterparts is that we grew up with the advent of modern technologies and political freedoms far beyond the comprehension of those who preceded us. As overwhelming to us as our recent history may be, we believe we have the capability to intervene in such a way as to change our destiny for better or for worse.

The ability of people to choose their fate is inherent in contemporary astrological prophecy. The issues and themes themselves seem mysteriously predestined to present themselves to us on the stage of life, but we may write the dialogue, and, perhaps, influence the outcome. It has been my personal experience that if we choose to ignore these cycles, history presents them to us in the harshest contexts. By making the decision to step up to the plate and embrace the search for the truth, we may be able to "invent" our way out of even the most profound set of challenges.

Time Lines

The chapters in this book are organized into time lines that are congruent with the slow-moving planets in the solar system – Pluto, Neptune, and Uranus. Although astronomers have recently demoted Pluto to a "dwarf planet", astrologers' observations since its discovery confirm this heavenly body as a powerful archetypal symbol. The Zodiac signs through which these planets move, important eclipses, their aspects (mathematical angles) with other planets and each other, symbolize the major issues and themes that will arise in our lives, and point to social, economic, environmental, and popular trends.

Every nation in the world has an astrological "birth chart" based upon the date, time and place of its birth, and the planets will thus symbolically interact differently with these contrasting charts. My primary concern in this book is with the chart of the United States that I prefer to use (July 4, 1776 at 5:10 PM LMT in Philadelphia, PA – see Appendix A), although charts of other nations will be frequently mentioned. For astrologers only, at the end of this book, I have included, important charts that I have referenced.

The ancient art of divination from the stars reminds us all that there are greater and grander movements in the universe than our limited intelligence can fathom. We cannot always be the originator of our collective fate, but we can decide to be asleep or awake when it unfolds. I think we have a better chance for survival, growth, and an extremely hopeful future if we are awake.

Chapter I

Pluto in Sagittarius (November 1995 - November 2008)

Globalization - Financial Speculation - Religion - Law - Education - the Media

Recent History

Since the turn of the 21st century, events have played out dramatically on the world stage in such a way that many people are dismayed, confused and extremely polarized about what it all means and what is destined to happen next. Once again, we are looking to the prophecies, both ancient and contemporary, to shed light on the landscape of history unfolding before our eyes.

1

Using the lens of historic planetary pictures, many astrologers have kept their clients informed of the challenging cycles all of us would have to face. In the process, these people have been able to conserve their financial assets, make appropriate investments for the future, and develop some understanding of the complex reasons behind all the undercurrents and hidden machinations going on in both government and industry.

My readers were warned that an act of war or terror would likely be committed in the USA between August 2001 and June 2002. My fear was, and still is, that the spread of severe economic inequities combined with religious fundamentalism would ignite global "holy wars," fueling ancient ethnic hatreds.

Astrological charts pointed the way to revealing that there was and is an increased likelihood that many corporations and financial institutions would be indicted for illegal practices. My clients were cautioned about enormous federal budget deficits, stock market fraud, lack of policing by the government, giant corporate pension and personal debt, and what Warren Buffet recently called the financial "weapon of mass destruction," unregulated over-the-counter derivatives.

Many people have had investment opportunities that have been highly successful because they have been adequately informed by astrological indicators of the kind of economic cycles that are with us now and that lie ahead. In 2002, my suggestions included heavy positions in precious metals, especially gold, energy stocks, potable water companies, "green" industries, and organic farming and food markets. I foresaw the massive loss of jobs to overseas "outsourcing" and encouraged my clients to move toward self-employment, pay down their debt, re-educate themselves, and live carefully within their means. My clients were encouraged to move inland to a place of elevation, with plenty of clean water and farmland. My readers have been warned comprehensively about living on islands or coastal regions, due to cycles of rising ocean waters and increasingly severe weather conditions. They have been cautioned that we are nearing the end of the "Age of Oil" and that we need to engage in the monumental challenge to find new and comprehensive sources of energy.

In addition to warnings with regard to the economy and, perhaps more importantly, I have been concerned about our society's frequent abandonment of compassion, concern for others, and an acutely critical awareness of what has been going on in our rapidly disappearing democracy. Pres. Dwight D. Eisenhower's words from 1961 ring out in my memory: "Beware of the military-industrial complex!"

The Age of Transition

As I study the positions of the planets, I am profoundly moved by this historic moment. We are at a crossroads in time in which two decisions are possible. We can allow an elite group of powerful people behind the scenes to manipulate economies, politics, and the world's precious resources to suit their personal purposes, or we can wake up, claim our rights to self-determination, and create new economies based on shared prosperity and a more equal playing field. With a new and heroic resolve, we may rescue our planet from economic, moral and ecological ruin. Awaiting us on the other side of these most challenging times, I speculate that there lies an expression of human civilization greater than all our imaginings!

Globalization, Finance and Trade

> *"The end of democracy and the defeat of the American Revolution will occur when government falls into the hands of the lending institutions and moneyed incorporations"*
>
> — Thomas Jefferson

Jefferson must be turning over in his grave. The number of corporate lobbyists in Washington considerably outnumbers the number of legislators. Most of us are aware that the Congress is absolutely inundated by money from the most powerful and wealthy special interests. Attempts to fix the system have, so far, been weak or ineffective. The McCain-Feingold Campaign Finance Reform Bill passed by Congress a few years ago is so watered down from its original, noble text as to be practically meaningless. The two-party system has rapidly become one party: the party of big money.

Pluto in Cancer (1914-1939): History seems to be repeating itself within new contexts, and with a new generation at the helm. The 1920s were a *laissez faire* capitalist's dream, with a huge population of working poor people and the largest percentage of America's wealth held by the elitist and powerful upper class, often referred to as the "robber barons." This eventually led to extremes of speculation in the stock market and the disastrous "crash" in 1929 resulting in the Great Depression of the 1930s, the worst economic collapse in U.S. history.

Pluto in Leo (1937/9-1958): The 1940s ushered in WWII, propelling us out of the Depression and building an unprecedented infrastructure of American industries. In 1944, the famous Bretton Woods Conference set out a gold-backed dollar as a post-war international reserve currency for international trade. The GI Bill and investments in public education paid off in vastly improved education and opportunity for Americans, creating an academic and scientific miracle that led us into space. The Korean War highlighted our new "Cold War" with Communist nations, primarily the Soviet Union and China, and vast amounts of taxpayer money went into both a conventional military and nuclear arms race.

Pluto in Virgo (1956/8-1972): In the 1950s and 1960s, America expanded into an enormous military and financial empire, uncontested economically due to the destruction of many nations' economies following WWII. The Marshall Plan invested in rebuilding the economies of our former "enemies," creating new markets. There seemed to be endless supplies of oil and gas to fuel this expansion, and European and American corporations successfully gained control over these assets. Cold War anti-Communist politics led us into the Viet Nam War. The Civil Rights Movement in the U.S. allied itself with an anti-war movement. Rev. Martin Luther King Jr., Pres. John F. Kennedy, and Sen. Robert Kennedy, leaders in these movements, were all assassinated. African Americans were granted full voting rights as citizens and we left Viet Nam. We continued to expand our investments in science and space. This was topped off by our landing astronauts on the moon, which was considered by many to be one of our most spectacular achievements.

Pluto in Libra (1971/2-1984): The 1970s brought with them extreme oil price inflation, recession and job losses. The Federal Reserve imposed high interest rates in an economy historically characterized as "stagflation." In 1971, the U.S.A. was unable to back up its currency due to the massive inflationary policies of the 1960s, and the dollar was taken off the gold standard. Pres. Richard Nixon resigned from office when threatened with impeachment amidst the Watergate scandal. Worst of all, the U.S.A. reached "peak oil" within its own boundaries and thereby lost control of oil pricing. The ouster of the Shah of Iran (an American ally) and the installing of an Islamic theocracy there enhanced the long conflict with the Middle Eastern nations, their historic and increasing hostility to our ally, the nation of Israel, and uncertainties for the future price and availability of oil. For a time, under the leadership of Pres. Jimmy Carter, we switched to more fuel efficient cars and began research projects on alternative energies that were, tragically, almost abandoned in the decades following. (See astrological chart for the birth of an Islamic Iran at Appendix B.)

Pluto in Scorpio (1983/4-1995): In the 1980s, our government removed or allowed to expire many of the regulations on banking and corporate governance that had been in place since the Great Depression. Computerization and automation led to greater efficiency. Credit and debt began to expand, as did the economy. We observed the "junk bond" scandals, a stock market "boom and crash" and, due to a fall in the price of real estate, had to face the failure of many savings and loan institutions by the early 1990s. These failures were ultimately paid for by the U.S. taxpayer. Due to heavy military spending and tax reductions for large corporations, we incurred large budget deficits leading us into recession. The "Cold War" with the former Soviet Union ended, the Berlin Wall fell, as Pres. Ronald Reagan worked with Russian Premier Gorbachev to end the hostilities. This led to the breaking up of the old Soviet Empire and left the U.S.A. as the reigning economic and military superpower.

In 1995, Pluto entered the sign of Sagittarius (1995 – 2008). In the 1990s, one of the biggest stock market "bubbles" in U.S. history, led by the now defunct "dot.com." companies, was further inflated by the "creative accounting" cheaters led by Enron, World Com, Global Crossing, and some of Wall Street's most prestigious brokerage houses. The temporary profits gained from the advent of the internet technological boom coupled with rising taxes on the richest Americans enabled Pres. Clinton and the Congress to pay off the budget deficits, leading to budget surpluses. Knowing that control of

Eastern Europe and their crucial oil pipelines was essential to the continuance of our control over energy assets, the U.S. and NATO involved themselves in a civil war in Bosnia, bombing the Serbs into submission, and establishing a military presence there.

Bye-bye Jobs! So Long Middle Class! Tax Breaks for the Rich.

Since the passing of the NAFTA global trade treaties in 1993, corporations have been free to "outsource" millions of American jobs and set up factories in countries like China with a cheap and unorganized labor force and few if any environmental restraints or costs. Many of these same corporations have evolved into international holding companies that have frequently been able to avoid paying taxes by creating offshore accounts and have made so much money that they are able to control the media, the markets, and to an alarming extent, the U. S. legislature. As a result, tax breaks have been legislated for the already wealthiest Americans.

In addition, it has been increasingly easy for large corporations to avoid paying taxes. Common Dreams.org New Center recently (Feb. 25, 2007) published an article originally published by the Inter Pres Service entitled "Corporate Profits Take an Offshore Vacation" by Lucy Komisar. She writes: "Last week, Merck, the pharmaceutical multinational, announced that it will pay 2.3 billion dollars in back taxes, interest and penalties in one of the largest settlements for tax evasion the U.S. Internal Revenue Service (IRS) has ever imposed. Merck had cooked its tax books by moving ownership of its drug patents to its own Bermuda shell company – an entity that has no real employees and does no real work – and then deducting from U.S. taxes the huge royalties it paid itself." She goes on to quote IRS Commissioner Mark Everson from last June: "Tax issues associated with the transfer of intangibles outside the United States have been a high risk compliance concern for us and have seen a significant increase in recent years. Taxpayers, especially in the high technology and pharmaceutical industries, are shifting profits offshore."

Our budget crisis has led to the "spin" that we must dismantle programs like Social Security, Medicare, Medicaid, etc., that provide safety nets and help sustain the middle class and the poorest members of society. Already federal cuts in funding for education, highways, and other infrastructure necessities have brought many individual states to the brink of bankruptcy, forcing them to raise local real estate and sales taxes, which disproportionately affect the poor and the middle class.

All this has resulted in many people questioning why they should have faith in an economy so complex and subject to manipulation that the average person is barely able to comprehend it. A culture of endless consumption has evolved along with the culture of endless credit and debt. This, combined with the enormously expensive war in Iraq, is resulting in the greatest government budget deficits in history and the largest personal debt for American families ever recorded.

Rather than spreading the wealth of deregulated markets around and raising the standard of living of the poor, instead globalization has made a relative handful of people very rich while poverty is increasing in the U.S.A. Decent jobs are becoming extremely rare, and the middle class is becoming a threatened species. As I write this book, exposures of government lobbying scandals, insider trading, illegal trading, and corporate fraud are an ongoing occurrence. However, the "spin" continues that we are in a great economic "expansion." I would like to ask: an "expansion" for whom? Recently, after a disappointing performance, the CEO of Home Depot left with an exit package of over $250 million. At the same time, there is a great protest on the part of corporate capitalists to raising the minimum wage that has not even been corrected for inflation since 1996.

Public Infrastructure?

In the May 8, 2007 issue of *Tom Paine.common sense*, author Sam Pizzigati in his article: "Coming Soon to a Toll Booth Near You" exposes how our roads are being sold off to corporations, no longer benefiting the public at large. He points out that there is a general movement over the past several years by governors and state legislatures to sell what we used to call the "public infrastructure," mainly our highway system, to large corporations. This helps them avoid tax increases on the rich, often thought of as political poison. As a result, there would be no accountability for the corporations to pay the money to maintain these roads, tens of thousands of full-time government jobs would be lost and replaced by part-time employment with no benefits, and tolls could go up to unsustainable prices, especially for truck drivers and others who make their living on the highways. He calls our attention to the fact that Democratic Governor Ed Rendell is privatizing the Pennsylvania Turnpike and last year, the State of Indiana gave private investors a 75-year lease to run the Indiana Toll road. He says: "The next two years, *Business Week* predicts, could see '$100 billion worth of public property' turn private."

America's Greatest Strength - The Will to Dissent

More recently, there has been a gathering force of opposition to these forces, a public outcry for change, and a renewed interest of citizens in their democracy and their cherished rights. Books are being written and published by courageous people with levels of expertise few of us have been able to acquire, and we need to pay attention. After a virtual hiatus from real investigative journalism, many are now demanding an accounting from the powers-that-be, uncovering deceptions and bringing out truths that have been languishing in the dark for years.

In the November 2006 elections for Congress, the public expressed its desire for change by giving the Democrats a majority in both houses. However, the public-at-large frequently seems to be either disinterested or overwhelmed, or both. Circumstances will change all this and people will literally be forced to face these realities!

In his book, *Perfectly Legal (The covert campaign to rig our tax system to benefit the super rich – and cheat everybody else)*, David Cay Johnston states: "In 1977, the richest 1 percent of Americans had as much to spend after taxes as the bottom 49 million. Just 22 years later, in 1999, the richest 1 percent—about 2.7 million people—had as much as the bottom 100 million Americans. Few figures derived from the official government data on incomes present more starkly the growing chasm between the rising incomes at the top and the falling incomes at the bottom."

The Congressional Budget office stated in 2004 that the income gap in the United States is now the widest in 75 years! While the richest one percent of our population saw its wealth grow 109 percent from 1983 to 2001, the bottom two-fifths watched as its wealth fell 46 percent.

We have lost nearly 4 million jobs overseas and the number of jobs outsourced to India and China is growing every month. Illegal immigrants are pouring into the country, taking jobs that pay a pittance. The combined effect is the lowering of the level of wages paid in this nation to a point of seriously endangering the existence of the middle class in America! Recently, we have witnessed public protests on both sides of this issue. So far, no substantial change has been made that would reverse the tide.

The people who occupy positions at the top of the food chain are appearing on television telling us, "Outsourcing is good for the country and it actually creates jobs in America. We only need more education (another threatened species) in math, the sciences and technology."

As the money for public education, especially in lower income areas, is on the decrease and operational expenses to run school systems is on the increase, young American people are lacking basic skills and scoring low on tests of crucial math and science compared with other nations. Even more alarming is the fact that 2.2 million Americans are now in prison, most of them young, poor and from racial and ethnic minorities.

Where's the Economy of Main Street?

Pluto in Sagittarius has opened the doors wide for privileged elites who were positioned to take advantage of investments in the global economy. These people send their children to private schools and live in gated communities, insulated from much of the decaying infrastructure outside. Meanwhile, the so-called average American citizen is losing health insurance, highway and infrastructure repairs, access to decent public education, affordable colleges, adequate numbers of policemen, firemen, and a host of necessary people who make it possible for the local governments of states and cities to function. Local property and sales taxes on middle class citizens are rising incrementally in relationship to the federal budget deficits brought on by the war in Iraq, the growing number of people retiring and tapping into Social Security and Medicare, and tax breaks for those people in the wealthiest two to five percent of the population. The march to "unequal opportunity America" continues unabated. Meanwhile, our elected officials in Washington have been busy as bees legislating to protect the interests of corporate lobbyists and others who contribute large sums of money to their campaigns.

Reverse Robin Hood

It is starkly obvious that we have played into the hands of powerful manipulators who can do so because the legal checks and balances installed after the Great Depression of the 1930s have been allowed to expire, be ignored, or quietly removed from corporations and financial institutions. Laws have been passed to regulate these entities, but they are not being enforced because Congress has not delegated funds to hire the people these government agencies need to enforce the law. Some would say our government is now: "In the pockets of oligarchies," reminiscent of the monopolistic, non-tax paying robber barons of the early part of the 20th century.

Huge global corporations, most which originated in the U.S., have effectively decoupled themselves from America and its historic national commitment to the rule of law. Many of these same insiders in the 1980s and the 1990s had developed and enhanced the policy of "dollarizing" the world, forcing down the price of gold and allowing the tanking of other currencies. Recently, gold has risen and the dollar has fallen, indicating a change in influence on the part of the global financial managers. More recently, even as the dollar fell further, these same clever controllers keep trying to tank gold once again with the hopes that people would not race into gold as a protection against the falling dollar. The fluctuations in gold prices back and forth are reflective of a loss of confidence in the dollar, fiat currency in general, and the future of the U.S. economy.

The average U.S. citizen, who is encouraged to invest in financial markets, has little or no information about these powerful and behind-the-scenes machinations. Meanwhile, an increasing number of countries alienated by U.S. government and corporate policies are forming their own alliances and coalitions. Central and South American nations, recently influenced by Venezuelan Prime Minister Hugo Chavez, are moving to the far left and away from governments allied with U.S. corporations. China and India are forging oil deals with Russia and Iran. The war in Iraq has imploded into a civil war and is threatening the stability of the Middle East, moving these nations away from American influence. Many countries are positioning themselves to be considerably less entwined in the interests of the U.S.A. (See Appendix L for an astrological chart for Iraq on June 28, 2004 when the U.S. transferred power to the government.)

Place Your Bets!

The blatant (and perfectly legal) wildly accelerated use of derivatives as a financial instrument is allowing large and small financial institutions (hedge funds) to participate in a highly speculative, roulette-wheel style of economics.

Derivatives are instruments based upon values derived from other markets of value. They are contracts or "bets" on the prospect of the changing value of anything; stocks, mortgages, commodities, interest differentials, even weather. The term *hedging* is the ability to assume potential losing positions in the hopes they would be covered by winning positions somewhere else. Fans of derivatives are convinced that the increase in the use of these instruments helps to decrease overall economic risk toward the people who can afford to assume it. These participants are taking risks they are trying to offset with derivative contracts from someone else.

What so many people do not realize is that since about 1995 (when Pluto entered the sign of Sagittarius) a likely catastrophic economic "bubble" has been secretly forming in the over-the-counter derivatives market. If you can contact parties who are willing to bet against you, you can get into the derivatives market as a speculator. To make matters worse, you only have to put down a fraction of the amount you wish to bet so, if you lose the bet, you may be liable for much more than you put into it. If you buy a stock for $25 a share and it goes down to $15, you can still sell it for $15, taking a $10 loss on your original investment. If you buy a derivatives contract that is a "call" or bet the stock will go up, and that stock goes down, you can lose more than you originally paid for the contract! In addition, these contracts have frequently become so complex that they have become nearly impossible to understand, let alone regulate.

This type of trading has been going on for years within limits, and had its place as a constructive "hedge" against potential losses, especially in the price of commodities. However, in recent times, the amount of global derivatives trading has escalated beyond the stratosphere. These instruments were behind the 1987 stock market "crash," the 1997 Asian currency crash, the fall and failure of Barings Bank in 1995, and more seriously, in 1998 the failure of the giant hedge fund, Long-Term Capital Management, nearly causing the collapse of the entire global financial system. More recently, the infamous and widely publicized fall of Enron was connected with their severe losses in derivatives trades.

The risk during the recent past does not even touch the enormous risk that has ballooned at this historic moment. J.P. Morgan Chase has now become the largest gambler in history with a "notional" derivatives portfolio at the time of this writing of somewhere over $49 trillion. It was last reported in 2006 the global "notional" derivatives trade was somewhere around a staggering $370 trillion! The term "notional" is used because the value in these contracts changes from second to second and cannot actually be determined until the option expires or is exercised. These figures are periodically published by the Bank for International Settlements.

The Fate of the Dollar

Since the end of World War II, the U.S. dollar has been preeminent in the global capitalist economy and is the major currency in world trade. This has stimulated the world to buy into U.S. Treasuries to the point that foreigners own more assets in the U.S. than Americans own in other nations, now approximately 43 %. Within the last two decades, America went from being the world's biggest creditor to the world's biggest debtor. This has enabled the government to get away with irresponsible policies that are supposed to hold back economic recessions by expansionary fiscal policies and lower interest rates without affecting investor's faith in our currency. The truth is that government debt is at an all-time historical high, household debt (mortgages and credit cards) is astronomical, while household income has not increased substantially along with corporate profits. Most recently, the last bastion of help for the people, the safety nets (Social Security and Medicare) are now at risk. The looming question is: what will happen to our economy when other nations lose faith in our economy and exit the rapidly falling dollar?

What Retirement?

The current administration wants to allow young people to put a percentage of their Social Security into investments that would pour more money into the pockets of rich Wall Street financial firms and corporate stockholders. In actuality, the vast majority of young people know little or nothing about the financial markets, let alone the laws (or lack of them) that regulate the industry. The money young people pay into the system finances those who have retired and are currently collecting their benefits. It is as plain as the sky above that this proposal would most certainly take the "security" out of Social Security. What would happen to these assets during a crash such as the ones in 1929, 1987, 1973 and 2001? In addition, there are serious questions being raised about the Social Security Trust Fund being filled with what many people refer to as IOUs for the money that is "borrowed" to fund other parts of the budget.

Bad corporate governance in recent years has stimulated "dipping" into pension funds or simply not paying into them at all to help their profit margins and the price of their stock. The net effect is that of reducing the benefits, or abandoning them altogether and turning them over to the government. The big "secret" is that the government is simply incapable of funding this large a pension deficit. The truth is that the so-called "retirement asset" for the Baby Boomers has been seriously reduced for all but a tiny elite of highly wealthy individuals.

The Culture of Debt

Credit and debt have been necessary to create the vast and mostly successful American economy and are axioms of the modern capitalist system. However, a Culture of Debt has been practically institutionalized in our society as the average household in America has taken on increasingly large mortgages, second mortgages and startlingly high chronic credit card balances. Back in 2004, Prof. Ellen Warren of Harvard University informed us that since 2000, the number of foreclosures on homes had risen by 45%. She pointed out that many people have been allowed to take out adjustable rate mortgages at very low rates, not realizing that these rates could rise to the point where the borrower may be unable to pay. We are now just beginning to feel the pain of the escalating rate of foreclosures as the result of the frenzy of sub-prime lending over the past several years. The April 25, 2006 issue of *Bloomberg News* reported that mortgages entering foreclosure jumped 72 per cent during the first quarter from a year earlier. This was all before the recent radical decline in the housing market. The inevitable implosion in the real estate market alone could be devastating for the country.

As employment in America becomes increasingly fragile, and the costs of housing, energy and healthcare escalate higher and higher, people who have little or no savings run up their credit cards just to pay their bills. Thus, they are subject to sudden increases in credit card interest rates, and are frequently forced into declaring bankruptcy. The most recent legislation on bankruptcy, successfully lobbied in Washington by the credit card companies, now eliminates the ability to seriously reduce or eliminate the debt of the struggling middle class person who has been devastated by serious illness or job loss.

The Decline of Steady Employment

With the passing of the NAFTA Trade Agreement, corporations have jumped on the opportunity to ship the labor needs of American companies to India and China, reducing wages due to the considerably lower standard of living in these nations. As soon as the workers in these countries start demanding a higher wage, the corporations have the option to move out of these regions as well. This leaves nations unable to finance their infrastructures and provide education, utilities, health care, and basic living accommodations for their people. Again, this illustrates the "decoupling" of corporations with nations, divorcing them from responsibility for the devastation they frequently leave behind, i.e., unemployment and poverty.

Current government reports showing low unemployment in America discount the millions of people who have given up their job searches and are depending upon family members to support them. You are counted "employed" if you have a part-time job with no benefits, or your unemployment expired. Many who lost good jobs in manufacturing and the computer sciences are working in retail industries at minimum wages that cannot support them. Others have attempted to start their own businesses and have produced no income for years, but are listed as "employed" because their unemployment has run out.

One of the most profound changes in the national economies may be long-term structural unemployment! The recent transit of Uranus in Aquarius (1995 – 2003) symbolized the climate of enormous growth of technological innovation, including the widespread use of cell phones, personal computers and the advent of the Internet. The "automation that will replace people" feared since the 1950s is now reality. In America, we have historically defined ourselves in terms of productivity in the workplace. As we are being replaced by machines and displaced by "outsourcing," it is obvious that the consequences will be so dire that we desperately need a new economic model. The need for new leadership in the USA will be required; someone who thinks "outside the box" of traditional political conservatism or liberalism.

Over the past twenty-five years, there seems to have been an abandonment of the concept of checks and balances so revered by the writers of our Constitution. There also seems to have been an abandonment of the notion of healthy competition and a more equal playing field. Many people who are "in the game" have abandoned ethics, morality, and, most of all, the will to look at the consequences. Corporations exist for one reason only – to make as much profit as possible. It is up to governments to regulate and restrain, forming checks and balances on otherwise unrestrained financial power concentrated in the coffers of the very few.

Global Politics, Oil and War

The tragedy of 9/11 and the recent war in Iraq follow years and years of cultural, religious and economic power struggles in the Middle East over the existence and power of Israel and the control of oil. Recently formulated policies of using the mighty military of the U.S.A. to evoke regime change and completely control this region for the oil companies has alienated much of the rest of the world and effectively destroyed the peacemaking and diplomacy-driven foreign policy of the U.S.A. that has existed for the past fifty years. At the time of this writing, we all now know that Iraq has descended into a holocaust of fragmentation and civil war. This tragic mistake will evoke serious consequences throughout the region for many years into the future.

In his powerfully compelling book, *Confessions of an Economic Hit Man*, John Perkins describes his personal odyssey as an economic "numbers-cruncher" for an international consulting firm and covertly, an agent of the U.S. National Security Agency. His job was to promote the interests of a coalition of U.S. government, banks and corporations, enabling them to make billions of dollars while frequently devastating both the economies and the lands of people in developing nations. Deals were made with the local heads of state, offering them bribes and encouraging them to borrow copious sums of money from the International Monetary Fund, seriously indebting their nations. The IMF loan money was automatically transferred into the accounts of American corporations for infrastructure changes, enabling the oil companies and other corporations to set themselves up. Frequently, if a head-of-state refused to cooperate, he was "mysteriously" ousted in a coup, died in an accident or, as a last resort, the U.S. invaded his country. An example of this, he states, was the CIA-backed ouster of the democratically elected prime minister of Iran in 1951 when "Iran rebelled against a British oil company that was exploiting Iranian natural resources and its people." The result of this was the installation of the pro-American Mohammad Reza Shah, whose repressive dictatorship resulted in the Iranian Islamic coup, installing a government that remains hostile to us to this very day. Other examples were the elimination of President Omar Torrijos in Panama and the CIA overthrow of Chile's democratically elected president, Salvador Allende. He points out that this policy of unchecked economic imperialism, especially in the nations of the South America and the Middle East, has led to the hatred of the U.S. and the tragic attack of 9/11 on America. Without sparing himself, he outlines years of the use of these practices and their dire consequences on the economies of native peoples and their environment.

Recently, the President of Venezuela, Hugo Chavez took advantage of the widespread hatred of the U.S. and allied himself with our old enemies, Cuba and Iran, while launching a public relations campaign all over the world against the United States. In the past, Chavez would have appeared ridiculous. Today, the present American administration has antagonized so many nations that he is viewed as a hero by many and has become a mouthpiece for the far left.

The Saturn/Pluto Opposition of 9/11

Between July 2001 and June 2002, Saturn (the establishment) formed an opposition with Pluto (crisis, death and rebirth) on the ascendant/descendant axis of the chart of the United States. In early 2001, a number of astrologers (myself included) predicted an extremely high probability of a terror attack or military confrontation in the U.S.A., based upon the history of previous harsh connections between Saturn and Pluto. This tragic event has led us into a policy of global war and our current leaders have presented to us no clear-cut way to either win it or end it. The Bush administration convinced the Congress and many Americans that Iraq had weapons of mass destruction, we invaded, and now we have a black hole war in this nation that has plunged the country into an ongoing Hell, subjecting our brave young men and women to seemingly endless internal factional conflicts.

Recently, the democratically held elections in Iraq presented some hope that efforts would be extended toward cooperation rather than war. However, the nuance and understanding of the history and cultures of the Middle East is noticeably absent in the American presence there, as the recent disastrous insurgencies demonstrate. It is becoming clear that occupation by our forces is a primary reason for these violent upheavals and that destabilization of Iraq has promoted ancient ethnic and religious hatreds. In addition, the scandals pertaining to prisoner abuse and torture are clearly demonstrating we have crossed the line in implementing this war, which is in violation of the Geneva Accord that America itself helped to forge! Recently Pres. Bush has introduced legislation designed to exempt America from following this standard.

By staging this preemptive war, America has seriously alienated most of the other nations of the world, undone peace and disarmament treaties forged by previous American administrations over the past fifty years and seriously undermined the United Nations, the only all-inclusive international diplomatic forum in the world.

We will have to face the fact that recent policy is only the latest in a long series of wars since World War II in which the United States has involved itself and that we have been more than willing to use our increasingly scary military might to impose our will on other nations, either for their natural resources or to serve some vague cold war policy. Like the Roman Empire before us, we are in danger of going bankrupt financially due to the escalating costs and losing face as we incur the hatred of much of the world at large.

In the July 2-8, 2004 Issue of the *L.A. Weekly*, Prof. Chalmers Johnson of UC Berkley, and the author of *Blowback* and *Sorrows of Empire* wrote: "We have 725 military bases in 138 foreign countries circling the globe from Greenland to Asia, from Japan to Latin America, self-perpetuating military bureaucracy rather than a rational strategy. The greater cost is what the public will lose if they haven't already lost it: the republic, the structural defense of our liberties, the separation of powers to block the growth of a dictatorial presidency."

In 2006, Johnson published his third book in this trilogy: *Nemesis: The Last Days of the American Republic*, in which he thoroughly explores how a permanent military economy, saddled with crippling debt, a loss of our democratic freedoms, and generalized resentment abroad will likely lead us toward the same fate as the Roman Empire before, taking us into bankruptcy and a general collapse. The astrological configurations ahead suggest a high probability of such a future if we do not intervene soon to take back our republic.

Clearly, it is imperative that we face the fact that a primary reason for the 9/11 attack on America was the stationing of U.S. soldiers on land in Saudi Arabia after the Gulf War. The reason for the insurgency in Iraq is the on-going occupation of U.S. soldiers in their country! On March 2, 2007, *Platform Press Release* reported: "Iraq's cabinet has just approved a Hydrocarbon Law which will allow foreign companies control over Iraq's oil for the first time in 35 years."

Oil - Here Today and Gone Tomorrow

As in the 20th century, the first half of the 21st century will be defined by the competition for dwindling oil and gas reserves throughout the world. At this time, a major and potentially volatile struggle for Russian and Caspian oil has begun as China and India enter the fossil fuel race and the principal sources that lie in Kazakhstan, Azerbaijan and Turkmenistan. Georgia, Ukraine and Afghanistan are absolutely necessary in the equation since they contain the pipelines through which the oil and gas can be taken to the international markets, bypassing Russia and Iran. Through NATO or direct military presence, the U.S. and Europe are seeking to safeguard these regions and their pipelines. All of this points to the strong probability of decades of struggle throughout the world in order to control the remaining oil and gas deposits.

Now, in addition to the enormously unpopular war in Iraq that gets worse day by day, killing Americans and Iraqis because "insurgents" resent occupation by America, and their government is too weak to control religious and ethnic factions that continue to fight each other, we are building the same case that was proven false in Iraq, to stop nuclear development in Iran; i.e., that they are making weapons of mass destruction. If they are, we have lost the ability to do very much about it since our military personnel and financial resources are being drained away by the Iraq war.

Religion and the State

Pluto in Sagittarius during 1995 – 2008 points out that religious fanaticism is rearing its head once again, deepening the historic wounds from centuries ago, and compelling us to revisit ancient battles we thought were long finished. It is startling how little progress human beings have made psychologically and spiritually as we fight wars over religions whose originators preached tolerance, love and peace.

The rise of Muslim extremists producing large numbers of suicide bombers and fearless terrorists is an extremely complex phenomenon that cannot be simplistically reduced to phrases like "enemies of freedom." I seriously doubt that Osama Bin Laden choreographed the 9/11 attack on the World Trade Center because he was upset about the Bill of Rights. (See astrological chart for the 9/11 attack at Appendix C.) As stated above, it may have had something to do with American military forces stationed in Saudi Arabia and this administration's disengagement with the Israeli/Palestinian peace process that has now fallen into ruin.

The nations of the Middle East have been unable to make a transition from a tribal pre-industrial economy into modern times. Their gigantic oil wealth has been exploited by Western democracies, making a handful of tribal monarchs enormously wealthy, while leaving most people in near hopeless poverty. Religion gives them a personal dignity and some kind of hope for a better life in this world or the next. Many people see Americans as exploiters of their resources, usurpers who disrespect their culture, and are absolutely allied with their hated enemy, the Israelis. Their young men eventually are easy recruits for sociopaths like Osama bin Laden and murderous terror groups throughout the region. These subcultures of Islam use their religion as an excuse to commit mass murder and multiple suicidal bombings. The insurgents that are attacking in Iraq are part of a historic agenda of extreme religious and ethnic intolerance.

Back in the U.S.A, the neo-conservatives in Washington had assumed an extremely cynical foreign policy, adopting the scary philosophy of Machiavelli; i.e., that "the ends justify the means," a philosophy present in all fascist regimes. This philosophy also condones lying to preserve the state's power and preemptive war to achieve their ends. These wars are allegedly designed to "convert" nations to the notion of freedom and liberty, so cherished by our nation. This present regime was supported by sizeable populations of evangelical Christians in the past two presidential elections. A substantial number of some particular sects of Christianity believe the end of the world is at hand and Jesus Christ will shortly return to take these particular evangelical Christians up to Heaven in the so-called "Rapture," while the rest of the non-Christian world sinks into a dreadful apocalypse. In addition, "weapons of mass distraction" have been used by politicians that highlight issues before the electorate such as gay marriage, stem cell research and abortion. These issues are certainly worthy of discussion but will have no relevance whatsoever if current policies in Washington lead us into escalating wars and eventual economic collapse.

As I am writing this book, scandals are rocking Washington, especially in the Republican Party and there are conflicts arising from the "Evangelical Christians" as to whether they have supported candidates who really represent their beliefs.

Simultaneously, and most ironically, the Patriot Act in the U.S.A. is taking away liberties guaranteed by the Constitution, such as the right to be formally charged with a crime, the right to legal counsel and the right to a trial, just as Pluto in Sagittarius (religion) squares Neptune (idealism) in the horoscope of America. The Bush administration has declared itself to have the right not only to tap our phones without a warrant but, more recently, to open our mail without a warrant. There is even a threat to the balance of powers so sacred to the writers of our Constitution, as religious extremists in Congress seek to interfere with the independence of our judicial system as in the highly publicized Terry Schiavo case. The past two presidential elections have even raised serious questions about the authenticity of computerized balloting and the very safety of the election process.

Religion and Government

The question at hand is this: Are institutionalized religions simply a version of ancient warring tribal cultures, exploited by governments and/or terrorists for their interests, or does each one of them contain a pathway to peace, harmony, and a more evolved spiritual sensibility? It seems that humanity needs to participate in something spiritual more than ever before, and yet many of the old formats seem destined for self-destruction.

As I am writing this book, there are serious crises in most of the world's great religions. The Israeli-Palestinian struggle over land and statehood has become a seemingly endless Muslim vs. Jew conflict. The attack launched by Osama bin Laden on the U.S.A. is an extension of this. The on-going problematic relationship between Pakistan and India is largely Muslim vs. Hindu, particularly played out over the control of Kashmir (which has sadly recently suffered a devastating earthquake). The 1990s genocidal massacres and war in Bosnia and Kosovo involved the ethnic clashes of Christians vs. Muslims. The planet Pluto is symbolic of crisis, the abuse of power, death and destruction. Sagittarius is a sign associated with religion and the law. This placement of Pluto in Sagittarius has ignited the ancient "holy war" idea, and has revealed the dark side of religion-as-a-tribe, defending itself against another tribe whose opposing "God" has to be defeated. Ancient practices many thought we had outgrown are rearing their heads again in the 21st century.

In the U.S.A. over the past twenty years, we have seen the rise of fundamentalist Christianity into the political arena, bringing up historic and constitutional questions as to Church vs. State. Recently, the scandal around sexual abuse in the Roman Catholic Church has shed light on the very structure of government within the church, its propensity to cover up wrongdoing, and its relevancy to modern societies.

The death of Pope John Paul II has reminded us of the yearning of so many people for spiritual leadership and equally of the long and historic string of controversies behind it. The election of the new Pope Benedictus XVI has reaffirmed the ultra-conservative direction of the Roman Catholic Church.

The Importance of Religion

I am of the opinion that what is needed is not to abandon religion, but to give up our narrow, childish interpretations. We need to move away from blind adherence to authoritarian hierarchies grounded in fear, whether ancient or modern, and claim responsibility for our own essential spiritual growth. This requires of us a willingness to examine our personal lives, our society, and the direction humanity seems now to be taking. The rise of the dominance in our culture of a veritable worship of the almighty dollar (the religion of unregulated "plutocratic" capitalism) is giving birth to an authentic hunger for spirituality. People are truly searching for a meaning to their lives that goes beyond the Dow-Jones Index and NASDAQ.

Perhaps religion can become a means to expressing reverence for the beauty of nature, life, and the unknown, respectful of science rather than being at odds with it, and respectful of diverse traditions rather than being repelled by them. With an open mind and a loving heart, all pathways could lead to enlightenment. The essence of each of the world's great religions is a respect for the dignity of life, an ethic of sharing, and a love of peace.

My Prophecies:

Politics and the Economy

Even though there may be new highs made in the stock market in 2007, economic deprivations will deepen and darken, increasing poverty, violent crime, bankruptcy and homelessness. More jobs may be added to the economy but they will be primarily government/ military jobs, low-wage service jobs, temporary employment, and positions outsourced to cheap labor forces in other nations. The recent increase in jobs has been fueled largely by employment in the real estate sector whose "bubble" is starting to lose momentum.

Although the stock market may project some optimism, the economy of Main Street will not get better for most people, especially in the employment and earnings sector. With Saturn in Leo from July of 2005 – September 2007, the economy has temporarily seemed to improve in some sectors and we may reach new stock market highs. Saturn opposes Neptune during this period (August 2006 – June 2007) and the powers-that-be will likely attempt to bring down the price of gold, oil, and other commodities, hold the line on interest rates, and temporarily stem the tide of inflation. Nonetheless, in the latter part of 2007, dollar inflation will rear its ugly head as oil and gas prices increase, forcing interest rates upward.

The March 19, 2007 solar eclipse square Pluto symbolized increasing problems with oil exporting nations, and escalating violence. Between September 2007 and March 2008, the theme of war and terror will rise once again with an increased probability of another attempt to attack the U.S., as Mars transits Gemini and opposes Pluto in September of 2007 following a solar eclipse on the fated September 11ᵗʰ anniversary. Since Mars will go retrograde, it opposes Pluto again in January 2008 and March 2008, symbolizing violent clashes and disagreements. In addition, there may be a major currency crisis brought on by the derivatives trade.

By comparison, the period of early 2007 is a short-term "up" cycle in the financial markets, compared to the much longer-term bearish cycle that will inevitably play itself out from 2008 through 2026, and discussed in later chapters.

The End of the Age of Oil

Throughout 2005 – 2008, as Pluto opposes the U.S.A. Mars and squares the U.S.A. Neptune, we will be forced to confront the price of our dependency on foreign oil, especially as the price of oil and gas fluctuate in the extreme, the above mentioned competition around the globe accelerates, and we recognize that much of the world's oil lies in countries that are politically unstable. There will be discoveries of new oil and gas sites, but the consequences of rapid global warming due to the accelerated use of fossil fuels will have to be confronted by governments on a worldwide basis. We will be compelled to face the fact that the "age of oil" that has fueled our modern civilization is coming to an end!

Inflation, in spite of powerful government and banking institutions' attempts to control it, will raise its ugly head as energy prices continue to remain high and increase the cost of doing business everywhere. Continual dangers of terrorism and war will force us to collectively examine the reasons behind all this. Political ideology and media spin will no longer succeed in masking the covert reasons for our military involvements in the Middle East. We will realize that rather than the U.S.A. effectively "democratizing" these regions, they will rally around various religious sects. These nations, once destabilized by conflicts with each other, may begin to disintegrate from within. Many of these countries, including the State of Israel, were formed in the years right after W.W.II, when Pluto was in Leo. Transiting Neptune in Aquarius is forming tense aspects with their charts, pointing to weakness in leadership and an environment of chaos and uncertainty not seen since the early 20ᵗʰ century.

The Future Is Green

The good news is that higher energy prices will motivate us to invent and drive electric "hybrid" gas-saving cars, build solar houses, erect windmill farms, and stimulate new investment in new energy producers such as bio-fuels, hydrogen technologies, nuclear plants, and other alternative to fossil fuel energy sources. Already, people with money and resources are making serious investments in this direction. Some examples are billionaire Richard Branson's commitment to developing alternate fuel sources, Robert Redford's foundation for renewable energies and Al Gore's media campaign in the movie *An Inconvenient Truth*. The environmental movement, seriously pushed backward in recent years, will gain positive momentum both politically and economically. British Petroleum (BP) has already made a sizeable investment in solar technologies. The nations of Europe are putting up giant windmill farms. Brazil has recently invested in the bio-fuel industry, making itself "energy independent." Here in the U.S.A., where we should be leading the world in the renewable energy and environmental movements, we have helped subsidize big oil by driving big gas-guzzling cars. This trend has already begun to change as orders for fuel-efficient and hybrid vehicles are on the upswing. The auto companies are designing new cars moving toward electric vehicles. In addition, California recently passed an initiative to bring solar technology into the erection of public buildings. My projection is that we will be forced to dramatically change our ways much more quickly than originally planned. We will have both opportunity and motivation to *invent our way out of the crisis.*

Who Is to Blame?

This same aspect will force us to look at our fears that the world has become a dangerous and hostile place. The question is this: Is the danger coming from outside forces, especially Middle Eastern nations that have reason to hate us, or is the danger coming from within our very own corporations, financial institutions and government insiders using our economic good faith as their Devil's playground. In short, is the enemy out there, in here or both?

Most of all, we need to abandon the "living in fear" mentality and enthusiastically embrace new ideas, new leaders, and a renewed faith in our ability to rise to the historic occasion. If we allow ourselves to be intimidated by our current government that has recently passed a law that allows citizens "suspected" of collaborating with terrorists to be whisked away to a secret prison without the right to be accused, defended and tried in court, we will certainly be finished as a democracy.

From 2005 – 2006, Pluto in Sagittarius opposed Mars and squared the Sun in the horoscope of the U.S.A. Constitution, challenging its authority and the rights and liberties it has guaranteed all Americans. Whether it is the text of the Patriot Act, the right of the NSA to "wire" Americans without a warrant, changing the rules in the Congress around approval of judicial appointments, or issues surrounding the rights of people suspected of crimes, we must be vigilant that this great historic document is not compromised. Be aware that even an individual citizen's right to own property is now in question. In 2005, the Supreme Court in *Kelo v. the City of New London* upheld for the first time the use of "eminent domain" for private corporate developers, giving the local government the right to force us to sell our private property for use by corporations!

During September 2007 – October 2009, Saturn will transit the sign of Virgo, the sign most associated with healthcare, employment and the workforce. It will oppose Uranus in Pisces and inconjunct Neptune in Aquarius from November 2008 – September 2009. These very harsh aspects will symbolize an escalating rate of unemployment, a virtual capitulation of the healthcare infrastructure, a possible flu pandemic, a probable volcanic eruption in the Cascades and, coupled with the "crash" in derivatives markets at the end of 2007 and early 2008, could lead us into a cycle of serious economic depression by 2010. Fiat currency will be in real trouble, leading many countries and individual investors into the only historically stable investment; and that is likely to be gold. In addition, many nations who have accrued enormous amounts of debt will be teetering around total fiscal insolvency.

Scandals Unmasked

Here in the U.S.A., a series of scandals involving the government and the present administration will surface as Pluto continues to square the Neptune in the chart of America. In addition, transiting Neptune will pass over the Pluto in the chart of the U.S. presidency. In the past, the activation of this sector has coincided with danger to the U.S. president. This degree was occupied in Nov. 1963 by the transit of Saturn in this degree square transiting Neptune. We all know this coincided with the murder of Pres. John. F. Kennedy. March 19, 2007, Mars reached this degree, opposite transiting Saturn in Leo. A solar eclipse on this date at 28 degrees of Pisces square Pluto in Sagittarius symbolizes the exposure of lies and criminal behavior. Scandalous arrogance and tyranny may be uncovered on the part of people in high positions of power. These degrees will be activated by transiting Mars (violence and aggression) in September 2007 and again in the period between January – March 2008. We will become painfully aware that the lack of checks and balances instituted by our founding fathers has been seriously compromised and needs to be restored.

If there are still no regulations connected with the accumulation of a culture of debt and unrestricted use of over-the-counter derivatives, this could initiate an infrastructure collapse and Great Depression of a magnitude not seen since the 1930s. Between 2008 and 2009, we will likely be discussing a recession. By 2010, we may be talking about a "depression." It all coincides with the retirement of the Baby Boomers and pressure on Social Security and Medicare that, without intelligent reform, could collapse. At the same time, the oil and gas crisis will accelerate as the old oil fields in the Middle East reach "peak oil," ratcheting energy prices upward to insupportable levels.

Even though new oil reserves are being found in Africa and under the oceans, we will realize that even these will not begin to sustain the energy needs of world populations.

The trillion-dollar question for the 21ˢᵗ century will be the sovereignty of nations and the interests of the people versus the unregulated power of global banks and the dominance of multi-national corporations. Presently, giant corporations are making deals with local despotic governments, circumventing both the will and the welfare of the people. As noted above, this has been going on for years with the rulers of the oil-producing nations.

We will have to face the potentially suicidal consequences of state-sponsored capitalism placing short-term profits above the continuation of human life on the planet. As a backlash, socialism will increasingly gain popularity in the poor nations of Central and South America, as is currently happening in Venezuela. In addition, communism may make a comeback in Asia. Recently, Maoists are rising up in Bhutan, Nepal, and Indonesia. Presently, China is still technically a communist dictatorship that is allowing enormous capital market investment and rapid economic growth. When global markets crash, they will engage in a massive struggle with other nations, especially Japan and Russia, over the control of oil, gas and other commodities.

In addition, China will struggle with the consequences of environmental degradation and toxicity resulting from their unprecedented rapid rise of manufacturing and no laws restraining pollution, even though they are currently struggling to clean up their air and water. Global warming will exact its toll on this nation's resources, especially its water supply. The rapid rise of avian flu epidemics, combined with the seldom openly discussed AIDS epidemic will likely pose problems of great severity for this nation. Recently, laws have been proposed in China to protect the interests of labor. American corporations are trying to stop the passage of these laws because of the cheap labor they are able to hire.

I predict that international laws governing the environment, labor and human rights will have to be passed and adopted by the U.S.A. and other nations, and regulated and enforced by an international body. By August 2007, Saturn in Leo will harmonize with Pluto in Sagittarius, symbolizing a window of opportunity for this to begin. In addition, truths may actually come to light informing the public. The press, which has been negligently silent in recent years, may step up to the plate and expose the spin and the fraud that has been so prevalent for a long time. Here is where we have a clear choice to reverse the trend and head in the right direction.

How severely this cycle manifests depends upon the *con-scious choices* we make about the leaders we choose to oversee our destiny. If we continue our recent trend toward disengagement with the truth and ignore the freedoms, rights and privileges given to us by our democratic heritage, the consequences will play out in the theater of our lives. I am reminded of a billboard put out by the American Dental Association that said: "Ignore your teeth and they will go away."

Energy, Weaponry, and the Environment

As I began writing this book, the Defense Department requested that Congress give them the go-ahead to research the development of new "small scale" nuclear weapons, and in June 2006, a test was scheduled of a weapon of this type. This could easily signal other nations that, since America is moving in this direction, it is okay to re-ignite the arms race we thought was over when the Cold War ended. Recently, Vladamir Putin announced that Russia has a new and improved arsenal of weapons technologies that are "state of the art." There are suspicions that Iran and Syria are developing nuclear weapons technologies.

North Korea, as we all know, has recently publicly tested a nuclear weapon, bringing down the United Nations embargo on their already disastrous economy. Recently, we have agreed to go back to the bargaining table with them. China is arming itself to the hilt with new nuclear launching devices, sophisticated satellite technology, and state-of-the art conventional weaponry. At this crucial time, the U.S.A. is publicly stating we will go after groups and nations with weapons of mass destruction. Simultaneously, our very own military is increasing its own arsenal, reversing thirty years of disarmament policy. Information will likely be released that the U.S. has been using "spent" nuclear material, "weaponized" it in the form of "bunker busters" and contaminated regions of Iraq and Afghanistan with radioactive particles that our soldiers and citizens of these nations are breathing and ingesting. The public health, environmental, and political consequences of this new global arms race is simply beyond comprehension.

Finally, and perhaps most importantly, there may be the beginning of a series of *catastrophic climatic events*, most likely the effect of greenhouse warming. Additionally, we are entering a cycle associated with increases in earthquakes and volcanic eruptions. These events may result in temperature extremes, more frequent and more powerful storms, and other conditions so severe, whole populations may be displaced.

Recently, the Woods Hole Oceanographic Institute, arguably the most prestigious team of scientists in the world who study the ocean and weather patterns, has announced that the North Atlantic Oscillation is failing, and along with it, the Gulf Stream. For thousands of years, this has served as a "heat pump," moving warm equatorial water to the continents of North America and Europe. The failure is as a result of the melting of the polar ice caps inundating the ocean with fresh water, changing salinity levels as they have in the past, when mass extinctions of life occurred. The effect is to destroy the system of currents that equalizes heat and cold over the surface of the earth. Robert Gagosian, the director of Woods Hole recently said, "We may be approaching a threshold that would shut down the Gulf Stream and cause abrupt climate changes." A similar melting occurred, resulting in a 700 year-long Mini-Ice Age in Northern Europe and North America, as warming ocean currents disappeared during the Middle Ages.

On December 26, 2004, while I was writing this book, the greatest earthquake and tsunami in modern history claimed the lives of over 200,000 people. In August 2005, hurricane Katrina devastated the Gulf Coast and New Orleans, followed by hurricanes Rita and Wilma. Pakistan has just experienced a devastating earthquake in the area of Kashmir that has taken the lives of between 40,000 – 50,000 people. This is only the beginning.

Looking way ahead to the period of 2010 through 2014 (which I will discuss in later chapters), when Uranus in Aries is square (destabilizing) Pluto in Capricorn, we may experience serious earthquake activity and volcanic eruptions in many of the most populated areas of the world, including California, Indonesia, the Philippines, and China. The most recent catastrophic tsunami involving eleven countries in Southeast Asia reminds us how vulnerable populations are who have located their lives and economies in coastal regions. In addition, in 2010, under the grand cardinal cross involving Pluto, due to "peak oil" in many prominent oil-producing regions of the world, plus revolutions and "failed states" in many of these regions, we will likely run out of the easy accessibility to gas and oil that runs the infrastructure of our civilization as we have known it, possibly leading to a series of catastrophic oil wars.

If we do not prepare ourselves for these cycles, history's greatest chain of disasters for humanity will begin. If we have effectively switched to solar, bio-fuel, windmill and some new, yet-to-be-developed form of energy technology, we may be able to save ourselves and transform the direction of our lives. If we can move populations inland to places of elevation, and away from the coastal regions of the world, we may save millions of lives. If we are able to elect and empower an entirely new and elevated quality of leadership in our country, we may yet save ourselves from the worse case scenarios.

Inventing Our Way Out of the Crisis

Recently, in the January 9, 2005 issue of *Yahoo News*, it was announced that: "Researchers at the University of Toronto have invented an infrared-sensitive material that's five times more efficient at turning the sun's power into electrical energy than current methods." In an article by William Steenkamp in *Argus*, February 11, 2006, he announced: "In a scientific breakthrough that stunned the world, a team of South African scientists has developed a revolutionary, new, highly efficient solar power technology that will enable homes to obtain all their electricity from the sun."

Breakthrough research is being done at the Savannah River National Laboratory by the nation's largest collection of hydrogen experts. Recently, a new facility called the Center for Hydrogen Research in Aiken County, So. Carolina, is combining the talents of experts from governments, private industry and universities. Here are examples of the beginning of a cycle in which we may invent our way out of the coming crises.

In the November 27, 2006 *Guardian Unlimited Business* site on the internet, (http://business.guardian.co.uk) reporter Ashley Seager announced that: "Two German scientists, Dr. Gerhard Knies and Dr. Franz Trieb, calculate that covering just 0.5% of the world's hot deserts with a technology called concentrated solar power (CSP) would provide the world's entire electricity needs, with the technology also providing desalinated water to desert regions as a valuable byproduct, as well as air conditioning for nearby cities."

There are many new technologies, including biomass fuels, advanced solar panels, more efficient windmill farms, and the tapping of geo-thermal energy that lend hope for the future. More nuclear energy plants may be built, even though the problem of destroying toxic waste material has not been solved. I am of the opinion that an entirely new source of energy will emerge for which we have no current frame of reference. In addition, conservation will become widely practiced, and we may restore the electric train system for public transportation that we have seriously neglected in recent years, decreasing the need to use cars.

What can we do? I strongly advise people to move inland to higher ground where there are fresh water aquifers and rich farming land. The erection of solar houses (both passive and active solar systems) with water purification equipment, local organic gardens, and some kind of socially supportive neighborhood will direct us toward a sustainable and healthy way of life. (This is the pathway my family and I are taking, and ensuing chapters will elaborate on this.)

In addition, we need to support a major tax-shifting program to favor environmentally friendly and fuel-conserving industries. I believe our entire infrastructure of towns and cities in the USA will ultimately be transformed along these guidelines. I also believe we may create a more egalitarian form of capitalism on more localized levels, about which later chapters will elaborate.

Medicine & Health Care

There will be an attempt to reform the health care system in America as Uranus transits Pisces (2003 – 2011). However, the ongoing economic problems will increase unemployment and many more thousands of people will lose health care insurance. The losses in tax revenue will make programs like Medicaid and Medicare increasingly difficult to finance. The astronomical cost to doctors of medical malpractice insurance, the skyrocketing cost of medicine, and people's inability to pay will force us into a confrontation with the value system of business profits vs. human life. However, the burgeoning cost of the war in Iraq, coupled with giant and escalating government budget deficits, will severely limit what can be done. I predict that local and state governments will shoulder the responsibility and attempt to create their own healthcare systems.

Unless a great historic leader emerges in America to save our economy and redirect us away from recent policies, the Social Security and Medicare systems will be in danger of collapse between 2010 – 2014, much sooner than many of the pundits have told us. The gigantic budget deficits, the greatest since WWII, will continue to escalate into the black hole of Middle Eastern conflicts and the aging population "bomb" confronting us with the retirement of the Baby Boomers. In addition, many people may lose up to one half to two thirds of their own retirement funds in stock market crashes and corporate pension defaults.

Public pensions and both public and private health care plans throughout the nation will be under-funded and many will be fighting for their continued existence. Extremely high unemployment and low-wage jobs will inhibit money coming into those systems. Without good paying jobs, people can't pay taxes.

At the same time, there will be significant medical breakthroughs, especially in stem cell research and understanding how to combat viral infections. There will be real progress in the treatment and prevention of cancer. The recent bird flu epidemic and new flu viruses emerging will stimulate research in how to prevent animal to human transmission of infection.

Organic farms will be on the rise, responding to increasing demand for nourishing, nontoxic food. As Saturn recently transited the sign of Cancer (June 2003 – July 2005), people truly began to implement dietary changes in an attempt to prevent disease. Supermarkets that stock organic produce will be hugely successful. Simultaneously, however, hunger will increase in the U.S.A. as poverty increases. Access to health care will diminish on a worldwide basis just as the AIDS crisis accelerates and new contagious strains of flu begin to proliferate. The Saturn/Uranus opposition from November 2008 – September 2009 is the period of time for which we need to be prepared, as the potential for widespread illness will likely be on the rise.

The Media

There will be a historically important mighty struggle over the corporate takeovers of the media – newspapers, television networks, radio stations – and especially their more recent attempts to get control over Internet commerce. Whether or not we have freedom of speech, a free press, the right to openly dissent will be on the line. Many people feel that the last bastion of these freedoms is the World-Wide Web. If corporations are allowed to violate "net neutrality," as recently proposed legislation was intending they be allowed to do, the monopolies would win again.

Presently, a relative handful of people own and control the television networks, newspapers, magazines, big book publishers, and radio stations. Real news rarely gets to the public since the media giants are interested primarily in instant profits (advertisers) cutting costs, and pushing their own political agendas. Frequently, Americans have to resort to getting their news from foreign newspapers, newsletters and blogs published on the vastly expanding Internet. The combined power of the current administration in Washington and the giant media conglomerates results in really important information getting conveniently "omitted" from the public agenda. Some exceptions are C-Span, Lou Dobbs on CNN, PBS, NPR, magazines *The Nation* and *Vanity Fair,* and satellite radio programs such as Amy Goodman's *Democracy Now.*

More recently, a few mainstream news programs have had the courage to target real issues. Too frequently, however, people are avoiding either watching or reading about the news, feeling overwhelmed by all the tragic images and stories. The current administration is pushing legislation that would drastically cut funding for public radio and public television.

Eric Klinenberg, Assistant Professor of Sociology at New York University and author of *Fighting for Air: the Battle to Control America's Media,* was recently interviewed on C-Span. He described how the giant media corporations have eliminated local DJs and local news reporting, replacing them with generic mass-produced sound tracks, depriving cities and towns of their local news reporting, even in the event of local emergencies. He demonstrates how this is a profound misuse of the public airways, and that the corporate media is allowed to do this by the SEC and laws passed by the Congress allowing media consolidation. On the positive side, he points out that there has been a "grassroots" rebellion against this, resulting in the starting up of new local radio stations.

Highly respected media journalist Bill Moyers has expressed alarm in speeches, television interviews, and essays about corporate dominance of the media and its ensuing danger to our democracy. Reported on February 9, 2007 by the Associated Press, Anick Jesdanun wrote: "In a keynote address at Columbia University, (Walter) Cronkite said today's journalists face greater challenges than those from his generation. No longer could journalists count on their employers to provide the necessary resources, he said, 'to expose truths that powerful politicians and special interests often did not want exposed.' "

Between 2007 – 2008, issues will come up concerning accountability of the giant media monopolies. With Saturn in Leo, many of the people in high positions in the entertainment industries will leave or be deposed. Information may emerge that even the powers-that-be cannot suppress.

Chapter 2

Uranus in Pisces (March 2003 - March 2011)

The Quest for Beauty and Meaning - Social Disintegration and Redemption - Water, Drugs and Oil - Runaway Science

The last time Uranus transited Pisces was 1919 – 1928, and here in the U.S.A., we experienced the "Roaring 20s" in which young people threw out their inhibitions, speak-easies were born (as the result of Prohibition on the sale of alcohol), illegal smuggling of alcoholic beverages created millions of dollars for organized crime, Ford sold automobiles by the thousand, expanding the need for oil and gas, and what Americans thought was an endless "economic boom" was born.

Politically, one of the most significant events in human history took place. The Women's Suffrage movement succeeded in achieving the right to vote. Women threw out their corsets and bras (hence the term "flappers"), began to avail themselves of information about birth control, demanded sexual freedom, and entered the work force. We cannot even imagine the courage it took for these women to make the first significant move after thousands of years of virtual slavery, and begin a movement that has led to the freedoms and opportunities women have today.

Creativity boomed in America, with the birth of jazz, a significantly African-American music, and we witnessed the flourishing of some of America's greatest authors and playwrights. There were enormous Christian evangelistic movements sweeping across the country, with charismatic preachers and tent "revival" meetings. There was, indeed, a search for a primal creative force and a driving movement toward the search for meaning in life, whether through music, art, literature, or religion. In Europe and America, the emergence of the modern artists revolutionized painting. Filmmaking revolutionized entertainment, leading to the modern cinema.

The dark side of all this was rampant alcoholism, drug addiction, and social decay. The Ku Klux Clan organized and flourished as racism spawned hatred and violence. As a result of prohibition, crime became organized and escalated throughout America's major cities, trading on drugs, alcohol, and prostitution. Many people, not knowing what to do with their newly found freedoms, spiraled downward to self-destruction. The giant speculative bubble generated in the 1920s eventually led to the stock market crash of 1929 and the Great Depression.

In 1918, the World War I flu epidemic had run rampant throughout Europe and the U.S.A., killing more people than the war did. We had not developed an effective public health system to deal effectively with this catastrophe and some areas lost up to a third of their population.

The infamous "Teapot Dome Scandal" under the corrupt administration of President Warren Harding was exposed concerning shady oil deals involving the federal government.

Albert Einstein had recently published his Theory of Relativity and quantum physics was born in this era, revolutionizing science and our old and cherished beliefs about what constitutes reality. In 1925, the famous Scopes trial took place with religious conservatism challenging Darwin's theory of evolution. (Currently, this issue is being revived by religious conservatives promoting teaching "Intelligent Design" in public schools). This was an era of collisions between cherished notions and new discoveries.

Many of the old monarchies of Europe had been destroyed or altered by World War I. Adolph Hitler wrote *Mein Kampf* while in prison in Germany, sowing the seeds of a social insanity that would later lead to World War II. He capitalized on the economic and social disaster left by the war, extreme inflation of currency, and a weak Weimar Republic, offering up the Jews as a scapegoat and German racial superiority as a patriotic deity around which Germans rallied to create the horror of the Third Reich. In Russia, following the Revolution, communism had ruthlessly taken over the system of government. It is easy to see this era as a time of new experiments and social extremes.

Many other things of consequence happened in this era, not all attributable to Uranus in Pisces, and not all included in this brief historical retrospective. However, a picture emerges that could lead us to anticipate what lies ahead within the present time frame.

My Prophecies:

The Emergence of the Power of Women

The trend begun in the 1920s with Women's Suffrage and equality under the law in the U.S.A. has spread throughout western civilization, taking many steps backward and forward throughout the 20ᵗʰ century. However, the movement toward social and economic equality has not progressed in other parts of the world, especially in the poorest nations.

At this historic juncture, I think that *women will now fully emerge globally into positions of prominence and power.* I also think there will be a surprise in store for us, which is characteristic of the planet Uranus. The surprise will be women from the "developing" nations, who have been forced "behind the veil" into subservient positions for so long, will throw off their veils and assume not only full rights of citizens, but leadership positions in their various societies. They will likely accomplish this through expressing themselves and their ideals over the media. Women traditionally have looked at alternatives to war and terror to solve problems, and they may play a major part in creating the new social and economic systems we so desperately need at this point in history.

In 2003, an Iranian woman and in 2004, an African woman, each deservedly won the Nobel Peace Prize. Wangari Maathai, the 2004 winner is a leader and inspiration in the environmental movement. Recently, Ellen Johnson-Sirleaf was elected the first woman president of Liberia, Angela Merkel was elected first woman prime minister of Germany, Michelle Bachelet has been elected Chili's first woman president, and Portia Simson Miller is the new prime minister of Jamaica. The deputy prime minister of Spain is currently Maria Teresa Fernandez de la Vega, and a popular candidate for prime minister of France was Socialist Party candidate Segolene Royal. In addition, Phumzile Mlambo-Ngcuka is South Africa's deputy prime minister, Joyce Mujuru is Zimbabwe's deputy president, and Luisa Diogo was elected prime minister of Mozambique. Here in the U.S., we have seen Nancy Pelosi rise to Speaker of the House, third in line to the presidency, and considered the most powerful position in the legislature. Sen. Hillary Clinton has, as long expected, announced herself as a candidate for U.S. president.

For the past 2,000 years, many of the world's most prominent religions have been focused around male deities and hierarchies. There may be an acknowledgement of the strengths and abilities of women at this juncture in time that may transform our entire system of social and personal values. I think the most important result of this may be to *balance* the attributes of both men and women, emphasizing respect for one another and forming effective partnerships to solve the looming problems in the world of the 21st century.

In the 20th century, the election of Golda Meier in Israel, Indira Gandhi in India, and Margaret Thatcher in the U.K. have all preceded the movement here in America to place a woman in the top position. Women have been rising through the ranks in medicine, business and law and their numbers are slowly rising in the Senate and the House. We have had two women Supreme Court justices. Recently, we have had two women appointed to the position of Secretary of State. The numbers of women entering colleges and universities now outnumber the men. Within this seven-year cycle, we may begin to see men and women working together and all of society may benefit. The looming question will be: Will women simply imitate men, making the same mistakes as in the past, or will they forge new pathways to solving problems whose magnitude may be the greatest in human history?

The other great social revolution may focus on the rights of gay and lesbian couples. Recently, marriages of same-sex couples have been performed in San Francisco and a controversial court ruling in Massachusetts has granted this right. Our society is seriously conflicted about this now, but society was also in great conflict about whether or not to grant women the right to vote and, in the 1950s and 1960s, whether or not to guarantee African-Americans their rights as citizens. Many Americans were known to have registered their objection to gay marriage in the recent presidential election. However, the states are passing laws concerning civil unions that suit the populations of their regions. This issue will continue to remain prominent until 2011 when Uranus leaves the sign of Pisces.

Science, Medicine, and Technology

The last time Uranus was in Pisces, we witnessed our beliefs about reality turned upside down as quantum physics led us into the nuclear age, the space age, and the computer era. With the recent emergence of relativity, chaos theory, superstring theory, and even a theory that there is no time at all, our commonly held notions about what constitutes material existence may be nothing more than, as Plato foretold, shadows on the wall.

Biogenetic engineering and nano-technology will revolutionize medicine. There will be an enormous conservative backlash to this, as we have already witnessed in recent years, connected with cloning and stem cell research. Just as the Scopes trial was a debate between conservative Christians and Darwinian scientists in the 1920s, (which debate has arisen again

recently), there will be a debate about what constitutes life, as
new plants and body parts are engineered by us and introduced
into nature. As robotic micro-parts (remember *The Million Dollar Man*) are implanted in animal and human bodies, the dividing line between machine and living organism may become
less clear. Presently, there is even controversial research going
on involving combining human and animal genetic material. I
believe that the science fiction movies about the "takeover"
by aliens and their machines are a mythological projection of
the accompanying fears that surround these possibilities.

Another highly significant issue will come up for debate
and needs careful and lengthy consideration. That issue is the
capability for human beings to reproduce children outside of
the human body. Already, an egg and a sperm are combined in
an external medium and implanted in a mother's womb. This
procedure is viewed as fairly common today. If women do not
have to become pregnant and bear children, will they feel liberated or deprived of a great experience? Will a child, grown
in an artificial womb be psychologically and spiritually enhanced or seriously damaged? This scenario was explored in
Huxley's *Brave New World*, which depicted different types of
humans grown in giant containers and genetically engineered
into a kind of social caste system ranging from worker drones
to a privileged ruling class.

From time to time, we have looked at this frightening scenario, but are far from prepared for the social and moral implications of this capability. Recently, the furor over cloning has awakened debate about scientists, their capabilities, and where we stand as a society in restricting them. Between now and 2011, someone somewhere will achieve these things, whether we are prepared or not.

The replacement of body parts engineered from our own stem cells may lead us into an extension of life expectancy for which we are neither prepared socially nor organized economically. The present trend is to decrease the need for a human workforce through technology and to look for contract cheap labor in Third World countries. This will lead to chronically high rates of unemployment for most of the American people. It may lead us back into the caste systems of the past, i.e., a struggling, impoverished workforce, with a relatively small handful of wealthy and powerful people controlling most of the world's resources. How will we economically support a population that may expect to live 150 years? Will this medical technology be available only to the upper five percent of the population who seem to be holding most of the world's wealth? All this may be insignificant if we have an economic, social, and environmental collapse. Within that scenario, there would be no money or materials to continue these lines of research.

The Age of Biology

Author Jeremy Rifkin wrote in the Spring/Summer 2003 issue of *What Is Enlightenment?:* (pp17-18): "In addition to provoking serious public debate, the age of biology is going to raise the issue of how we define all of creation in a world where we can begin to reassemble it, manipulate it, redefine it, and organize it as a utility.

"We'll have to decide: Do we take a hard path or a soft path? Which means deciding: Will we use the new science to create a second genesis, to redefine and reconfigure millions of years of evolution, including our own, and, in a sense, play God? Or, will we use the new science to better understand the relationship between genes and environment, so that we can more fully – and more humbly, if you will – integrate ourselves into the first evolution on this planet?"

In the period of November 2008 – September 2009, Saturn in Virgo (health and medicine) opposes Uranus in Pisces and is inconjunct Neptune in Aquarius. I believe the long-imagined flu pandemic may emerge at this time. In 1918, Saturn opposed Uranus when the worst flu pandemic ever recorded spread throughout the world. Already, we are hearing about the spread of a particular avian flu virus in Europe, Asia and Africa. Much will depend upon our developing an effective vaccine and having the capability of dispersing it to the public. More importantly, we need to face the decline in our overall health due to an epidemic of obesity, diabetes and the ensuing complications of unhealthy diet and lack of exercise. Poor general health leads to a proneness to contagious disease. In addition, many people can no longer afford health insurance and have little or no access to preventative care. We cannot afford to put profit before human lives.

Environmental Changes

Pisces is a sign associated with water, oceans and aquifers. There will be a growing concern about the melting of the polar icecaps and startling reduction of mountain glaciers throughout the world. This is leading toward an inundation of coastal regions and island nations around the globe. In some areas, whole nations have been dependant upon mountain glacier water for their aquifers. This, combined with the intensification of heat, may turn many currently fertile productive areas into deserts.

In the July 19, 2003 issue of *The Guardian*, science editor Robin McKie reported: "Decades of devastation ahead as global warming melts the Alps. A mountain of trouble as Matterhorn is rocked by avalanches." The article goes on to say: "And in the future, things are likely to get much worse ... We have found that the ground temperature in the Alps around the Matterhorn has risen considerably over the past decade. The ice that holds mountain slopes and rock faces together is simply disappearing. At this rate, it will vanish completely – with profound consequences."

More recently in February. 2005, Dr. Tim Barnett of the Scripps Institution in San Diego, Ca. told the American Association for the Advancement of Science in Washington that he was "stunned" by the recent evidence of human-produced global warming due to the computer analysis of seven million temperature readings taken over 40 years to ocean depths of

2,300 feet. He went on to say: "The statistical significance of these results is far too strong to be merely dismissed, and should wipe out much of the uncertainty about the reality of global warming."

Al Gore's recent movie *An Inconvenient Truth* clearly both describes the coming emergency of global warming and inspires us to take up the cause of global environmental salvation.

Prof. Stephen Hawking, the famous physicist, astronomer and author of the best seller *A Brief History of Time, from the Big Bang to Black Holes* has recently publicly expressed his extreme alarm at the rapid rate of global warming which he sees as moving us toward extinction. He sees a global pandemic and nuclear war as the other two means by which we could be the means of our own destruction.

The recent dramatic acceleration of glacier melting in the Andes and western China could create deadly water shortages for millions of people who depend on this water source in these locations. The same melting will alter snow levels in the American mountain ranges, threatening water crises in the western United States.

Pisces is a sign that symbolizes liquids. As global temperature rises, scarcity of drinking water will begin to plague many regions and the search will intensify for underground aquifers. There may be conflicts generated between nations about who controls the water basins. Aquifers may become more valuable than oil wells. Presently, giant global corporations are buying up water rights, diverting rivers used by farmers for their crops, many of them located in the poorest areas of India and some African nations, depriving local populations of access to clean water and threatening their very survival. Ironically, many nations will be inundated with salt water as oceans rise. Some island nations may disappear altogether.

On the positive side, technologies for desalination of ocean water and water purification will be developed. Corporations and individuals who invest in these technologies will become very prosperous. We will become increasingly aware of industrial and chemical pollution of ground water and every household will soon own sophisticated water filtration equipment. Methodologies already being developed for the natural recycling of wastewater will become widely used and implemented by local municipalities.

Greenhouse warming will continue to bring increasingly alarming weather extremes and may cause displacement of populations, especially in Asia, Africa and Southern India. Island nations such as Japan, Bangladesh, Indonesia, Malaysia and nations such as the Netherlands, much of whose land is below sea level, may experience devastating floods and ocean water encroachment. Coastal regions in the United States, especially Florida, may wind up partially under water. The destruction of most of the tropical rainforests may cause the encroachment of deserts and severe scarcities of fresh water in those regions.

Most importantly, as mentioned above, unless we have major policy changes, I predict that by 2010, under a T-square of Pluto, Saturn and Uranus, we will be having serious difficulty getting enough fossil fuel to meet the growing needs of Americans, Europeans and the economically emerging nations, such as India and China. If we do not find an alternative source of energy before then, we may be looking at economic and societal challenge beyond our imaginings!

The Health Care System

Pisces is a sign concerned with the sense of compassion for the sick, marginalized and disabled. Uranus is a planet symbolizing innovation, technology and invention. Part of the reason for American corporate outsourcing of jobs is that companies can no longer afford the cost of health insurance, and neither can individuals who are self-employed. This is one of the greatest crises facing us today. We desperately need a single-payer health care system, saving money by a single, computerized, record-keeping system. However, Medicare is verging on insolvency and nobody seems to be doing anything really significant about reforming it and saving it. The pharmaceutical lobbies in Washington block any attempt at controlling costs of prescription drugs. The recent legislation including prescription drug reimbursement in Medicare is in serious trouble since the system cannot afford it and there was absolutely nothing in that bill to control costs.

I am afraid that America will be unable to create the system it needs in the near future because of the economic constraints that lie ahead of us. This country has made medicine a profit-taking enterprise, i.e., profits before lives. When we fully emerge from the economic crises ahead in 2026, solutions may present themselves to us and we will look back at this era and its failure to fix the problem as tragic indeed. In the meantime, as we go from global to local, governments of states and municipalities will likely design their own localized healthcare systems and solutions. There will also be a movement to computerize and consolidate information on the Internet to save the mounting costs of keeping and maintaining medical records.

Substance Abuse

People have used drugs and alcohol throughout history and it is only within the last couple of centuries that governments and societies have attempted to regulate them. In America, for about the past twenty years, legal drugs seem to be replacing illegal drugs, as we witness the rise of antidepressants, neural relaxants, and sleeping agents. Illegal drugs are still popular enough to be a big business and the ensuing addictions have continued to devastate the lives of millions of people for countless generations.

It seems ironic to me that we seem to know the least about the most important organs of the human body: the brain and nervous system. We may make major breakthroughs in medicine between now and 2011, shedding light on the electrochemical makeup of the nervous system, especially using techniques involving electrodes, light, sound, and magnetism. Genetically engineering new brain cells may be the treatment for Alzheimer's disease, depression, Parkinson's disease, schizophrenia, stroke, and other brain-related illnesses. We also may discover that many brain disorders are directly related to nutritional deficiencies brought on by our mass consumption of processed, chemically enhanced and refined foods.

In the 1920s, the speak-easies sold illegal alcohol to millions and substance abuse was rampant. We are doomed to repeat this unless we learn more about how to preserve mental health. Already, we are studying autism, depression, anxiety, panic attacks, attention deficit disorder and other nervous system diseases. Either more people are being diagnosed with these problems or more people are exhibiting these problems. As Uranus transits Pisces, a sign classically associated with all this, we may have to extend our search beyond medical science.

Spirituality and the Search for Meaning in Life

At the end of the Age of Pisces, we can look back at the development of the world's great religions as formats for social cohesion and frameworks for morality. They have presented to us pathways of openness, respect and reverence for all that is within us and beyond us. But we all know, like Cain and Abel, brother still kills brother and we fall far short of meeting the high standards for human behavior that these traditions have presented.

Frequently, religious organizations set themselves up as "absolutists, arrogantly condemning other religions as outsiders who can never hope to experience "salvation." Their interpretation of ancient scriptures is the "only truth." Their particular rites and practices are the only pathway to God. Dogma subsumes debate. Many of these religious cultures seem to be stuck in a kind of authoritarian hierarchical framework, reminiscent of the past and no longer applicable in a more egalitarian society with frameworks for open discussion.

Here in the West, a substantial number of people have been highly polarized, moving toward either dogmatic fundamentalism or an increasingly secular society, frequently abandoning our religious traditions as having failed us in some way. The problem is, *we* interpreted them so we have, in some way, failed ourselves! We need to be having more open debates as to why we seem to frequently abandon religious traditions of selflessness, concern for others, and sacrifice for a higher good.

Instead, we pattern our behavior after rock stars, sports heroes and billionaires, who seem to have replaced "the Gods" in modern culture. Everyone would agree that there is nothing wrong and everything right about prosperity. However, the selfish accumulation of personal wealth and power at the expense of family, friends, and society generates a kind of moral backsliding into times long past, returning to the same old historic tendencies of arrogant and insular ruling elites who have caused the failure of nations and abuse of their peoples many times before.

I believe the source of our greatest sorrows is an abandonment of personal spiritual quests, the loss of reverence for life, the earth, and the miracle of the universe. We have embraced, instead, fear, selfishness, and a veritable worship of gladiatorial competition.

My prophecy is that, in the future, as a result of a series of economic and environmental catastrophes, many people will move into a balance between the spirit of healthy competition and inspiring cooperation. Individuals will be encouraged to develop their unique talents and to work effectively in teams, sharing the ideas and the labor to get the job done, encouraging and supporting each other. Young people, weary of the selfishness of endless over-consumption, will move toward a society embracing cooperation with one another and working in concert with life here on earth.

As we move toward the Jupiter/Saturn conjunction in Aquarius in 2020, the age of the giant corporations and financial institutions will end, as a new intellectual and spiritual understanding penetrates the way we live economically. These institutions may be replaced by smaller localized regional micro-economies based on community, cooperation, and a sharing of resources, all having access to information on the World-Wide Web. Many of these resources may very well be local organic farms, with goods and services produced locally. People will no longer be estranged but will be reunited in their common goals. There may be an entirely new economic and social system devised, retaining private ownership and entrepreneurial incentives but sharing economic capital in a more egalitarian way.

As we develop a new consciousness that we are all part of the earth, the cosmos, and the sacred force of life itself, our behavior will change dramatically from operating in fear to cooperating with one another in the spirit of creativity and innovation. This will not happen overnight, but the need is accelerating to begin the process now. We may begin to examine what it means to us to be spiritual, and how that greater level of consciousness may be truly lived in our daily lives. We will discover that science and spirituality do not have to be at odds with one another. Francis Collins, the famous geneticist, has recently written a book, *The Language of God*, revealing his own journey into faith as a scientist.

Secondly, each and every one of us needs to open our hearts and minds to that which is greater and more open than our current and confining systems of belief. Whether we call this the scientific miracle of the universe, Allah, the Buddha, God, the Christ or the Holy Spirit, the human soul will wither and die if we continue to ignore what is perhaps the source of life, the meaning of life, and the very basis for the love of life. Eventually, out of this effort, a new global consciousness may be born. We will abandon a society that has tried to make us into either obedient slaves or working robots, and abandon a science based on things that have to be machine-like to be real. We may instead embrace the notion of personal authenticity within the framework of a life lived with meaning and purpose within the greater scheme of things. We may even discover through advanced scientific observation, a universe whose essence may be consciousness itself!

Another Reality

If you and I come to a realization on some fundamental level that we are all individual, living expressions of a whole universe that is, in truth, consciousness itself, we will, indeed, feel a "oneness" that has only been experienced intermittently by a few great avatars of faith. We may know, as many of the great poets, saints and theologians before us that there is no death; only transformation. We may, indeed, experience "the peace that passeth understanding."

It is my opinion that a major shift in human awareness will take place, just as the economic, environmental and social crises dramatically present themselves on the stage of history. This spiritual and heart-centered transformation will propel us into a realm of possibility far beyond anything we have ever previously conceived.

American Culture and the Arts

The last transit of Uranus in Pisces left a wonderful legacy of music, painting, writing and cinema that remains to this day a great source of enrichment and inspiration. Today, American pop media culture is a force driven by economics and is the most accessible to people. This is a mixed bag. What passes for art is often exploitive of people's worst tendencies, emphasizing sex and violence, strictly profit-driven. The other side of this historic expression has produced some of the finest drama and cinema in history. Great innovative architecture, new operas and symphonic works and modern paintings have been presented to us, but increasingly fewer Americans participate in or even know of these achievements.

In recent years, the public seems to have moved away from the fine arts in favor of pop music and the spectator sports arena. Entertainment and titillation seem to outrank inspiration. Alternatively, Public Television channels are available and many cable networks offer the viewer a few channels with enriching intellectual content. Sadly, more recently, the Bush administration has proposed major cuts in funding for Public Television.

In general, our culture is amazingly deficient in uplifting and inspiring people. Grandparents are showing up at concert halls and art museums, gazing around at other grandparents. Tickets have become so expensive due to the cost of financing these fine events that few people can afford them. Thus, many young people are not growing up exposed to the greatest cultural achievements of the past several centuries. The first things frequently cut from public school curricula are music and the arts, the very subjects that most inspire young people to be creative.

The good news is that we may see a new renaissance in the arts, a new kind of music, uplifting cinema and new and inspiring authors and playwrights. There may be a longing to revive the inspiring music of the last Uranus in Pisces period, the 1920s. There will be some kind of spiritual rebirth that will stimulate this movement. Modern technology in the entertainment industry is developing so quickly that it will help to implement this movement.

The quest for meaning in life referred to above may be a powerful incentive for esthetic expression not seen in many years. Major transformations in society and the modern framework for our lives will open new doors. This will eventually enable our children and grandchildren to bloom and flourish, standing in their own truth, in ways we have never dreamed of.

Chapter 3

Neptune in Aquarius (January 1998 - February 2012)
(Septile Pluto from 2001 through 2011)

The Ideal vs. the Evolution of Democracy - the New Community the Promise of Science - Society in Chaos

Community

The founders of our country inhabited thirteen colonies on the east coast of North America, living on farms and in relatively small towns. Families lived close together, and neighbors knew each other. A privileged few had traveled abroad but most people rarely ventured more than fifty to one hundred miles from where they were born. The Industrial Revolution was in its infancy and most people were self-employed farmers or merchants. Democracy and self-government were matters close at hand. The writers of our Constitution, intellectual outgrowths of the European Age of Enlightenment, understood that democracy would only work if the people were informed of the issues their elected representatives would decide. Their friends and neighbors were the ones going to Washington.

Today we are millions and we have spread across the continent. We come from every nation on earth, and every racial, ethnic and religious background. The average American family moves about every six years. We frequently change our employment, travel globally, and sometimes have more than one residence. Suburban sprawl is alienating people from a true "sense of place," experience of community or a feeling of responsibility for either.

Relatives who used to live together or in close proximity to one another are scattered all over the nation. Senior citizens live in retirement communities and see their children or grandchildren a couple of times a year. About fifty percent of marriages that take place today will be divorces within seven years. Families are splintered and relocated. Our neighbors are the folks we see when we put the garbage out once a week.

We have frequently lost touch with political parties, important issues and agendas. Often, we do not know who our representatives are, what legislation is being proposed or what has been passed into law. We have very little sense of neighborhood, community, or even our local landscape. People with a lot of money spend it to get people elected to an enormous, distant and complex central government, and the government furthers the interests of these people. These "special interests" have attained this power because we, the people, are too busy, and have all too frequently abdicated our hard won rights as citizens. My grandmother used to say to me, "If you don't mind the store, the store will be robbed."

Democracy is an endangered species. Community has become a group of houses and condos where we sleep and take a shower. Schools have frequently become places we deposit our children, express concern whether learning is taking place at all, and worry about the taxes we have to pay to support them. Many of us are so exhausted from working the long hours we are required to put in that we do not have the time or the energy to connect to the neighborhood around us, the needs of the school systems, or the local governance that determines whether or not the system works at all.

Our lives have taken on an incredible complexity within a vast societal framework no longer localized and comprehensible. Thus, we are waking up to our lives being controlled by the international global corporate giants and a government in Washington that frequently is no longer responsive to the needs and concerns of the public at large.

My Prophecies:

Back to the Future – Decentralization – From Global to Local

If we do not "come to" and take possession of our rights and privileges, this current way of life will experience an economic catastrophe just at the time the social time bomb of the Baby Boomer retirement goes off. Many people will lose their jobs, their homes, their retirement funds, but they will not retreat or give up. They will likely share households with family members or friends. They will have to regenerate local communities that work together to survive and perhaps even thrive. Local organic, communal gardens and the use of solar and windmill technologies to produce energy independent of fossil fuels will finally become a reality, leading us toward energy independence and local sustainability. A new discovery that at this point is completely unknown will be made, enabling us to create and store energy.

Shared childcare and elder care may all make a comeback within a new framework. That framework could be the "intentional community" that is economically healthy and environmentally sustainable. Real democracy may make a comeback as people vote for issues and community leaders who are close at hand and understandable. With local organic farming, advanced methodologies for recycling waste water, and the implementation of new non-fossil fuel energies, community can mean not only survival, but cooperation with each other and the natural world around us in a way that restores both biological health and personal satisfaction we rarely see today. The restoration of the local federalist form of government could reunite cities with surrounding towns, combining their utilities, saving money, and restoring efficient local governance.

This type of community could enable people to survive frequent unemployment, since it would contain its own micro-economy. Small but thriving entrepreneurial businesses may start up based on the model of mutual respect, teamwork, and creativity. Worker-owned companies may emerge as an alternative to governance by elites. People may still be connected to the world via television and the Internet, avoiding the age-old pitfall of isolation.

To implement all this, state governments and local governments of cities and towns will assume more and more control. Decentralization of power away from Washington will become a reality as the states battle the federal government in order to gain the power necessary to assume full responsibility for local governance.

You are probably shaking your head with disbelief at this point, thinking that the model for our lives in America in the 21st century certainly does not reflect this vision. You also may have realized that you are part of a society of people increasingly alienated from one another, increasingly insecure about jobs and sources of income, increasingly dissatisfied with the education their children are getting. You may also be among those who realize we may be heading toward both financial and spiritual bankruptcy!

The good news is, there are people who have given a great deal of thought and effort to these looming problems and have come up with unique proposals worth examining. Gar Alperovitz is a political economist from the University of Maryland and president of the National Center for Economic and Security Alternatives. He has written a book, *America Beyond Capitalism*, proposing a new social, economic and political system that would ensure and enhance democracy beyond its current crisis status. This system differs substantially from current models of both capitalism and socialism, pointing to the problems and inevitable declines of both, as there are abuses of power contained within each one. His alternative process is called a "pluralist commonwealth" that would establish community democracies with increased power of local government to make meaningful decisions. His ideas project new ownership institutions, including local, worker-owned companies and various national, wealth-holding institutions under the heading of a "Public Trust" projected to oversee the investment of stock on behalf of the public, the proceeds of which would go to individuals, states, municipalities to fund public services like education and healthcare. I would strongly recommend reading this book for it proposes solutions to the current abuses of power in both government and industry and suggests a more equal playing field. At the very least, this author is attempting to look for solutions beyond the current economic models.

Other creative and innovative proposals for the future are optimistically presented in the book *Natural Capitalism* by Paul Hawken, Amory Lovins, and L. Hunter Lovins. Social, economic and environmental interests are united in a new way, instead of being at odds with one another. A cornucopia of ideas is contained within this book that emphasizes corporate profits, the positive use of human capital, and a harmonious and environmentally sustainable way of life.

In 2005 – 2007, Neptune has been transiting 17 to 19 degrees of Aquarius, conjunct Pluto in the chart of the U.S.A. presidency (see astrological chart for the U.S. presidency at Appendix D). Important transits to this degree have been associated with serious dangers to the president, particularly notable during the terms of Abraham Lincoln and John F. Kennedy.

We have to be vigilant that extremists, in an effort to exert their power, do not subvert the democratic process. We will need to examine what we think constitutes leadership in our nation and who really controls policy. We will seriously look at any part of the government that is presently subverting the Constitution, taking away the right to dissent and the checks and balances that our founding fathers knew were of supreme importance to sustaining our democracy.

People will tend to distrust the federal government and, more and more, decisions will be made locally through state governments. As our federalist founding fathers did not trust the government in England, so the states will take more legislation and enforcement of laws into their own hands. Recently, Eliot Spitzer, formerly the New York State attorney-general and now the governor of New York, took the initiative of prosecuting corporate criminals. The State of Massachusetts has recently created its own healthcare system. Many states are scrambling to pass laws to override the recent Supreme Court decision on eminent domain. The State of California, followed by many other states, has passed its own clean air emission laws and the Bush administration is challenging these state laws claiming only the federal government has this power. Gov. Arnold Schwarzenegger is currently proposing a statewide healthcare system. This struggle between local and federal power is only just beginning. We will realize that our country has grown too massive to sustain real democracy, making it susceptible to the takeover by ruling elites. In order to take our democracy back, local governance will be on the rise.

As Saturn in Leo (despots) opposes Neptune in Aquarius (democracy), there will be great struggles among those who are in power, especially in India, Pakistan, and the Muslim nations in the Middle East. Israel will be especially torn apart by opposing factions within their own government and the continuing erosion around their borders. The struggle, on a worldwide basis, will be the ideal of democracy vs. the perpetuation of monarchies and despots. Put another way, will people prefer the "cult of personality" or the expression of the "will of the people"?

Democracy itself will be tested as people within nations become more polarized. Dialogue, dissent, and compromise are the hallmarks of successful democratic societies. These will all be sorely challenged as special interests refuse to retreat from their extreme positions. Ironically, just as Neptune (the ideal) transits Aquarius (democracy), real democracy is being challenged.

Within the broad context of human history, democracy, liberty, civil rights, a free press and personal freedoms are still new ideas. More recently, we have exchanged monarchies and dictatorships for plutocracies. Many people today see that governments are becoming increasingly irrelevant in the face of the money and power of corporations. Huge incentives for corporate heads to export jobs overseas to cheap labor markets are in place as they collect bonuses and stock options for short-term gains that will eventually destroy the consumer market to which they sell. The government as a check against this power has nearly been voted out of office.

Once again, the notion that "we the people" can create prosperity, have a clean environment, and do work that is meaningful and inspiring is practically revolutionary.

Agricultural Tyranny

One of the most horrifying examples of corporate power subverting the rights of local communities and farmers is the recent international effort of agricultural corporate giants to rob farmers of their ancient right to own and exchange their own seeds, forcing farmers, through seed patents, to buy only from them. Many people interpret this as an effort to establish a "seed dictatorship."

In her article February 14, 2005 in Znet, "The Indian Seed Act and Patent Act – Sowing the Seeds of Dictatorship," Indian author Vandana Shiva writes: "The Seed Act is designed to enclose the free economy of farmers' seed varieties. Once farmers' seed supply is destroyed through compulsory registration by making it illegal to plant unlicensed varieties, farmers are pushed into dependency on corporate monopoly of patented seed. She further points to laws passed in the United States: "In 1994, the Plant Variety Act was amended and the farmers' privilege to save and exchange seed was amended, establishing absolute monopoly of the seed industry by making farmer-to-farmer exchange and sales illegal." If a farmer purchases a "genetically engineered" patented seed from a corporation, he is not allowed to sell the seeds from his crops to other farmers. Apparently, all of this ensures the profits for the giant agribusinesses that are forcing small farmers out of business.

She continues at the end of her article to bring the point home: "Finally, without farmers' rights, there is no political mechanism to limit monopolies in agriculture and inevitable consequence of displacement, hunger and famine that will follow total monopoly control over food production and consumption through the monopoly ownership over seed, the first link in the food chain."

I predict that all of this will change, but it will only come about as the necessity arises. This rising necessity will come out of the consequences for a way of life that is no longer sustainable. The price of oil and gas has recently skyrocketed and is leading us toward an inflationary spiral similar to that of the 1970s. The already burdened middle class is being hit with higher heating and air conditioning bills, higher costs of health care, education and housing, all pushing them to rely more and more on credit cards. At the same time, the average wage has declined, bringing the middle class to the edge of extinction. There will be casualties. Whether or not you or I are casualties will depend on our choices now. Will we be destroyed or transformed? I choose to believe in the capacity in human life for transformation and enlightenment.

Until that full transformation takes place, many of us need to lead the way by framing or joining these new communities, creating new businesses with socially evolved working environments, erecting solar houses and windmills, preparing to grow our own food, produce our own clean energy, and creating new and inspiring systems of education for our grandchildren. We desperately need to share our historic experiences and *wisdom* with a younger generation who have cut their teeth on computer games, sound-bites and commercials; who have been inundated with information, but have precious little understanding of what it will take to survive. These children will have to learn about a workplace involving entrepreneurship, stewardship of the earth and its food chain, and the responsibility of self-governance. Schools may begin to teach students how to start their own businesses, build their capital, and govern themselves, making the basic skills they learn relevant to their lives.

On a more immediate basis, we need to develop and drive fuel-efficient cars, conserve our water, insulate our houses, plant an organic garden in the backyard. It is important to subsidize and invest in the entrepreneurs who are likely to come forth with new energy technologies involving solar cells, biofuels, and windmills, and other innovations in energy. We need to teach our children and grandchildren a profound respect for the earth, nature, and what we can do in concert with one another to conserve, and enhance rather than extinguish life on our planet.

Just as science and technology flourished in our educational system during the era of the "space race," we could interest our children in science all over again in the race to find and apply new sources of energy that are not from fossil fuels and solve the escalating problems of global warming and environmental degradation. Entrepreneurs who create companies to address these problems will flourish and stimulate economic development. The keyword to prosperity will be sustainability.

Most of all, we need to sit down with our families, friends and neighbors and have some serious discussions about how we will survive and thrive if the present system breaks down and fails us. How will we help each other get over to the other side?

The Future of Work and Financial Security

I grew up in America when a "work ethic" inspired people to find their "calling," i.e., a job or profession that fit their talents, interested them, made them money, and contributed to society in some way. In many ways, the notion that through hard work and determination, a person could climb up the ladder to both personal and financial success, has defined what many call "the American dream." Our country invested enthusiastically in waterworks, highway and rail systems, Social Security for the elderly and in public education for our children, knowing that this would result in a prosperous economy and a better life all around. Hard work was respected and personal excellence was rewarded. Getting rich was most people's desire but it was not a necessity. This was the "land of opportunity," envied by much of the rest of the world. It was a dream envisioned by our founding fathers.

Apparently, this was a "bubble" in the continuum of history that has again and again elevated a small number of peo-

ple into positions of power with huge stores of wealth, parti-
tioning the majority of people into a cheap labor force. During the Middle Ages in Europe, the appearance of merchants
created what served as a middle class, but most people were
still poor and disenfranchised. For thousands of years, national economies depended on surf or slave labor. The United
States fought a civil war over slavery as an economic institution that helped make plantation owners hugely wealthy. For
the past two centuries, the rise of democracy and free market
capitalism in America has spread to other nations and has
worked better than any other historic system. We are now in
danger of *reverting to these old partitions* as unregulated, global
corporations are seizing the wealth, opportunity, and power
we once shared.

For the past several decades, as job security has disappeared, instead of our young people looking for meaningful
work, many are looking only to magically "make money." This
is an extremely important shift in focus and is a movement
away from the idea of prospering through meaningful work
that contributes to the individual's well being and that of the
society as a whole.

Many people I have interviewed who teach in colleges and
universities are stunned at the lack of curiosity or interest on
the part of young people in literature, mathematics, science
and history. Instead, the students, when interviewed, are revealing they are there only interested in getting a degree as a
ticket to a six-figure salary in a multinational corporation. Di-

vested of passion for exploring a particular field, their motivations are frequently focused around money, consumption, and personal amusement. There is often a generalized disinterest in learning and a subtle disrespect for teachers in general, who rarely fall into the "big bucks" category. We cannot fully blame these kids, for this is the message our society has imprinted upon them at almost every turn. I am deeply concerned for these young people who are about to wake up in a time when their world will be turned upside down. Right now, the emphasis is not on workers but on stockholders; as if we just buy into the right companies, we won't have to worry about working at all. This illusion will shortly come to an end and the people who depend on it will be in shock.

A New Workplace

There are, however, a sizeable number of young people who *are* looking for truly meaningful work, invested with passion, spiritual inspiration and intellectual content. They are, in short, looking to design a future that is truly a departure from the one they are currently being offered. I have great faith in these young people to stand up to the challenges before them in these times and formulate a new workplace conducive to innovation, creativity and the free exchange of ideas. This will be in direct contrast to the secretive, cutthroat, competitive environment so characteristic of the monopolistic corporate environment of the past twenty years.

I hypothesize that a new generation, having suffered the collapse of the old system, will command systems of education that emphasize self-employment and entrepreneurship. The old model of assembly line, cubicle-style workers trained to obey a rigid hierarchy will likely come to an end. The sign of Aquarius is most expressive of innovation, democratically constructed teams, and a balance between healthy competition and group cooperation. The conjunction of Jupiter and Saturn in Aquarius in December of 2020 will be a marker for this change to take place.

Investments in a New Era

Over the past decade, many people have asked me the looming question: Where should I put my money? The uncertainties, and at the same time, the glamour of the notion of riches accumulated through investing in the stock market have seduced Americans in ways most of them have not examined and with consequences most are unprepared to assume. Financial markets are frequently influenced by networks of powerful corporations, government entities and financial institutions in ways that are often neither visible nor accountable to the public. The recent uncovering of the "creative accounting" cheaters and derivative market crashers has driven this point home to all of us.

Cycles fluctuate in ways that astrologers study and we can provide insights about the economy and the stock market within these particular time frames. However, the behind-the-scenes manipulators can leave all of us in the dust. In addition, the unforeseen collapse of a currency (such as the Chinese currency in 1997 and Russian currency in 1998) and the recent fall of the dollar, can throw everything up in the air. The unprecedented federal budget deficits, if left unchecked, could plunge our country into bankruptcy; an idea inconceivable just a few years ago!

Investment Recommendations

In the next few years, astrologers who study financial cycles and the astrological charts of individual stocks can be helpful to investors. Over the long term, I am recommending investing in a solar house architecturally designed for energy efficiency, in a "consciously democratic" community, inhabited by your friends and family, with its own localized supply of clean water, septic systems, organic farms and gardens, solar panels and windmills. Geographically, these areas need to be away from coastal regions, and well above sea level.

I also feel that investments in potable water stocks, water purification industries, waste recycling into energy companies, organic farms and supermarkets, energy companies, businesses that are developing bio-fuels, solar, windmill, electric auto and battery technologies are good places for your money. Gold and silver will rise in importance and value as currencies inflate or collapse, and I have been recommending this investment in my newsletters since 2002. Other metals, uranium, renewable energy technologies, are all good places to go in the immediate future. Although the metals and commodities may fluctuate in the spring and summer of 2007, we are in a long term commodities bull market. However, keep in mind that there are major uncertainties in the financial climate by 2008. As early as fall 2007, destabilizing events and crises are likely to drive financial markets downward and point the nation toward recession.

Remember that each company has good and bad governance, and large or small amounts of debt. Investing requires a great deal of work and constant monitoring. The public-at-large is startlingly unprepared and untrained in investing and this may account for the frequent failures of 401K plans that have taken over the pension plans that existed in the past. As far as mutual funds are concerned, the one consideration is the person or persons who are in charge of investing the fund and their historic track record. If the person with a profitable record leaves the fund and goes somewhere else, follow him or her.

Our major investment should be in a back-to-the-future community, run with modern technology, enhancing rather than degrading the environment and encouraging entrepreneurs to flourish within a system of healthy interdependence. These projects can inspire all of us to think outside the box and ask ourselves what kind of life we want to live and how we want to live it. These communities should move toward total solar architecture, the use of solar panels, windmills, and local hy-

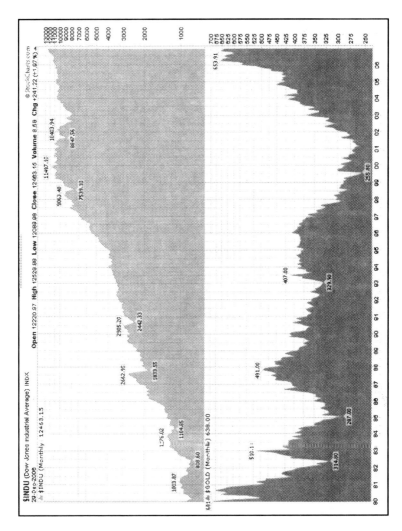

Upper chart: Dow-Jones Industrial Average from 1980 – 2007;
Lower chart: Price of gold from 1980 – 2007

droelectric power. Architecture to conserve energy will become hugely important to our entire society and will reframe the entire building industry.

My Prophetic Vision of the Future

I envision a future of small cities and towns, whose buildings are constructed by solar architects, surrounded by solar panels and windmill farms, supplied by adjacent organic gardens and aquifers that sustain the inhabitants, and will be managed by citizens.

Their populations will live in privately owned neighborhood cooperatives and will be thoroughly engaged in local democratic governance. Centers of art, science and culture will be available and affordable to all and will be at the center of interactive systems of public education that will no longer be alienated from but will be integrated into its economic and cultural systems. Entrepreneurship and creativity enhanced by protected individual rights balanced by effective and accountable group governance will bring us to the next level of the ideal of democracy.

Special Section - Easier Than You Think: The Solar Revolution

In *Basic Solar Concepts*, Donna K. Musial, AIA, describes specifically how we can either fully design or incorporate solar architecture and technology into our lives. She has written this section specifically to contribute to this book.

The sun, a renewable source of energy that has fallen in and out of favor in our modern society, holds a bright future for us. Today, as we search for ways to heal our planet, it holds answers that are not merely theoretical but are real, answers that come with consistently proven results.

While the energy and scientific communities occupied themselves with solar energy in the 1970s, few economic incentives were available to encourage its widespread and continued use in the public and private development. At the same time, political incentives encouraged continual reliance on fossil fuel. Entire solar systems that had been installed in homes or buildings by progressive entrepreneurs or developers in the 1970s and early 1980s were ripped out or abandoned not so many years later. The decline of solar was also not helped by the plumbing trade, which had not focused on learning to repair these systems. In their own way, many convinced their clients that solar energy simply did not work. However, they were then able to supply these clients with more conventional systems that use electricity or gas. Energy conscious homeowners have been frustrated by this for 20 years or more.

Today, however, there is increased interest in the use of renewable resources in most, although sadly not all, segments of our society. Widespread, thoroughly documented information shared by the environmental and scientific communities shows us that the sun is a viable and affordable source of energy. Proper use of sun-based systems will assist us in walking the tightrope of our immediate future in order to establish a balance in our ecosystems that will hopefully avoid catastrophic events. Solar energy in its many forms is definitely on the map for our future, both near and distant.

Solar energy is a term that encompasses a variety of systems. There are passive ways to use the sun that don't include the use of anything mechanical. Passive systems were used by our ancestors when the use of fossil fuel was not readily available and by our grandparents when mechanical air conditioning had not yet been invented. Homes built in the south with grand covered porches and large windows for cross ventilation between these porches didn't need air conditioning, yet were cool in the summer.

There are also very advanced systems based on solar photovoltaic power (PV) and solar thermal power. Although easier to install in new construction, some of these systems can be used in exiting homes. They are more affordable and available today than they were in the 1970s and can be purchased by a homeowner to reduce energy costs.

To build or retrofit a house to be totally dependent on solar systems is an engineering effort that should be undertaken with professional advice and oversight. However, while engineering/architectural expertise should not be ignored, it should not frighten the home owner into thinking small steps and maybe some big ones are not possible. "Starting in your own backyard" really does apply here in a literal sense.

Homeowners who do not choose to, or cannot move from, their present home to a home already designed with solar features can improve upon their present structure in a number of ways. Increasing the energy efficiency of the building envelope, interior and exterior lights and appliances is always the most cost-effective first step in this process. Immediate items of consideration should be:

- Installing a white reflective roof
- Providing additional exterior insulation such as in roofs or in outside walls
- Installing well shaded or reflective double-glazed windows where appropriate
- Use of ceiling fans in main zone to move air
- Landscape shading.

Knowing what system to use is important for conservation of money, time and effort. For example, it is impractical to use solar-generated electricity to heat water. A solar water heating system is a far more cost-effective choice. Solar features that should be examined before major upgrades to a home are made or purchased include:

- Use of passive solar heat gain and cooling
- Space heating from greenhouse heat
- Nocturnal cooling
- Use of thermal mass to temper the temperature swings in various house zones
- Solar hot water
- PV collectors.

Passive Systems

Since the sun is strongest and has the most solar impact from the south and west exposures, the orientation of the house in relation to the four directions is important. Obviously, an existing house cannot be moved, at least not very affordably. But, in hot weather, the homeowner can shield against the solar gain, and in cold weather, maximize it. Materials and designs such as the use of overhangs outside the house and landscaping can accomplish this.

The angle of the sun as it hits the building on the south and west sides of the home can be calculated by use of charts available from government agencies such as the EPA. The sun is high in the sky in summer and low in winter. Once the sun angle is determined during both seasons, overhangs can be installed. Where the overhangs are permanent structures, such as concrete brows or even panels, the exact length and width of the overhang will need to be calculated so that the high summer sun is intercepted but the low winter sun is allowed to penetrate to the windows and heat the interior. A more flexible but viable alternative is the installation of roll up awnings that are now manufactured to absorb heat gain. These awnings can be removed in winter.

Another passive method for reducing the solar gain in summer is to plant deciduous trees outside the north and west walls. Trees absorb heat, and deciduous trees for the most part in most climates will lose their leaves in winter. Evergreen trees can be used in the same way in parts of the country where winter cold is not a factor. The trees or vegetation act in the same way that an awning does – to shield the sun from impacting the windows and wall in summer and allow it to warm the wall in winter. Use of evergreen trees on the side of the house where cold winds blow, will further reduce the effect of the winds and lower heating requirements.

Windows on the solar side of the house need to be transparent enough to allow the sun to heat the home but block infrared re-radiation from inside to outside. There is a wide range of window glass types that will transmit light differently in various parts of the energy spectrum, such as in the visible and the infrared. Consideration should be given to whether both heat and light or only light is needed before a new window or window system is installed. Manufacturers' literature is plentiful on the products available.

With regard to the north side of the house, where cold needs to be kept out, the glazed window areas should be minimized. But, where provided, they should be double or triple pane designed for thermal efficiency. On the north side, the concept of thermal mass can be used to decrease loss of heat and allow heat stored in the thermal mass to radiate into the space when needed. The thermal mass concept is that building materials absorb solar energy at different rates and when a large enough mass is provided, the heat that is absorbed goes further into the material when the air around it is at a higher temperature. This will be the case if the sun is hitting it for any length of time. When the air cools, the heat stored in the material is released into the space around it. Thus, the use of insulated windows to absorb and release heat at a slower rate than the transparent windows.

If the homeowner has the space and resources to build a solar greenhouse, a great deal of energy could be directed into the home. A solarium is a sunroom with a large expanse of glass roof and walls that accepts sun and heats the space inside. The most efficient use of a solarium to produce heat requires that the solarium be on the south side of the house. If the solarium is set at ground level, it can be used to grow vegetables that are watered on a timed drip system. At the lower level of the solarium, a screen door or panels are installed which will allow colder air from the adjacent rooms to enter the solarium. The warmer air at the top of the solarium needs to be vented with damper controlled vents into the other portions of the house. The sizing of the screening and vents must be calculated to allow for proper air movement that will, for the most part, happen naturally according to the chemistry of air and the effects of heat. If necessary, ceiling fans can assist in the airflow.

Active Solar Systems

More active systems can be installed in the home to heat and cool as well as supply energy for electronic devices. With regard to hot water, solar collectors are simple, relatively affordable systems that can be installed as roof panels or ground level panels connected to a storage tank. When a swimming pool is also heated with the system, the swimming pool not only acts as a container to take excess heat from the water in very hot weather, but it also acts as a heat storage tank in cloudy weather when more direct solar energy cannot be used. Of course, the pool is covered with thermal blankets to eliminate immediate heat loss.

Photovoltaic Systems:

Often called solar cells, photovoltaics are semiconductor devices that convert sunlight into electricity. In very simple terms, the devices consist of usually two layers of semiconducting material, one negatively charged and one positively charged. When sunlight hits the cells, the radiative energy from the sun forces electrons from one side to the other and the resulting "energy" is captured to charge batteries, power electrical loads such as home appliances and operate motors.

One single cell produces 1.5 watts of power, which is insufficient for home use. However, cells are wired together into modules that are electrically connected to form a string. The strings are connected together to form an array of modules that can then be used to produce alternating current

(AC) compatible with any conventional appliance. These arrays can interconnect to the utility grid used by the major utility companies.

The energy crisis of the 1970s resulted in efforts to develop PV power systems that can be used for residential application. According to Florida Solar Energy Council, the production of PV modules has grown 25% annually in the past 5 years and major programs in the U.S. are facilitating increased growth beyond this statistic. According to the American Solar Energy Society, "the energy payback time (the time it takes the system to generate the same amount of energy that it took to manufacture the system) for PV systems is two to five years. Given that a well-designed and maintained PV system will operate for more than 20 years and a system with no moving parts will operate for close to 30 years, PV systems produce far more energy over their lives than is used in their manufacture."

The advance in PV technology has resulted in products available to current homeowners that provide alternatives or supplementations to conventional electric energy sources. The "solar shingle" is one of these products. The shingles can be applied in lieu of a conventional roof system when a new roof is needed. They look like the traditional shingles placed on sloped roofs, but because they are lightweight, the need for structural reinforcement of roof framing, in most cases, is avoided. The tiles do not use glass and are a durable product with conventional warranties. Other similar type products include Sunslates, which are designed to replicate slate roofs and fit to standard slate battens. Solar glass laminates provide both electricity and insulation, although more expensive at this time than the other two alternatives. The laminates are composed of layers of heat strengthened glass with an air space similar to double glazed windows.

If a homeowner does not want or need a new roof, panels of various sizes can be constructed of these materials to be placed over or above any portion of the existing roof to provide energy. With a little creativity, the panels can alternatively be used to give the effect of an awning or a new roof line to complement the home. To maximize efficiency, the best locations for these panels would be a south or west exposure.

Solar energy systems can be very simple or very intensive. However, with so many new choices, nothing stands in the way of homeowners starting today on the future course of conserving energy for tomorrow."

Traditional shading device on the south wall allows light but reduces solar gain

These window shading devices are retractable. They have three lengths and can be adjusted for different angles of the sun

Overhangs and vegetation also shade windows

Solar panels on a roof that visually blend into the shingles

Chapter 4

Pluto in Capricorn, Uranus in Aries, Uranus Square Pluto, Neptune in Pisces

The Establishment Becomes "Disestablished" – The American Revolution Part 2

The Rising of the Oceans

The period 2008 – 2024 corresponding with Pluto's passage through the sign of Capricorn, presents astrological patterns very much like the 1530s, (the Protestant Reformation in Europe and the ensuing religious wars), the 1770s (The American Revolution) and, with its square to Uranus in Aries, the 1930s (the Great Depression).

The famously publicized Maya prophecy, the end of their 5,200-year calendar cycle occurs during this period, ending exactly on Dec. 21, 2012 on our calendar. Interpretations of the real meaning of this period ending are difficult to discern since the Maya are no longer with us to explain what they meant. However, experts such as Bruce Scofield, MA, who has specialized in Maya astrology and was recently interviewed on the History Channel, sees this as a time of confrontation with the consequences our civilization has brought down upon itself. He comments: "The 'end date' of the Mayan Calendar (12/21/2012) should be understood more as a period of time than as a single date. It marks an important astronomical alignment between the winter solstice point and the galactic equator, an alignment that occurs roughly every 26,000 years. I think we need to give it a range of at least 20 years, before and after 12/21/2012. (See Appendix E for the astrological chart for the Winter Solstice of 12/21/2012.)

"It might also be thought of as a 'beginning date.' For the Maya, life is cyclic and this point in time marks the completion of the previous cycle and the beginning of the next.

"Whether or not this alignment is actually 'causing' changes is not known, but it does seem to coincide with conditions of global urgency (over-population, scarcity of resources, climate change, etc.) caused by humans. The coincidence of this alignment and the current conditions on our planet are striking. We should regard it as a monument to the astrological sophistication of the ancient Maya and as an opportunity to understand what we have done to the Earth."

Just as significantly, during this time frame, the sun at the Winter Solstice December 21, 2012 coincides with the Vedic (Hindu) astrological cycle symbolizing major endings and beginnings for humanity. The *Vedas* are four volumes of incantations and rituals from ancient India that scholars think were written around 600 B.C. The *Upanishads* contain philosophies and mythologies that are thought to have been written between 800 B.C. and 400 B.C. The actual prophecies are contained within the Hindu *Puranas* that designate our current time period as the "fourth age" or the Kali Age of darkness and conflict. At the end of this age of destruction, their savior God, Vishnu, returns to take humanity to a more evolved or higher plane of existence.

All these prophecies are remarkably consistent with the story, yet to be told, of how humanity will face the age of transition from endings to beginnings.

Let us look at the realities we may face.

Economically, as I have said in previous chapters, these patterns suggest that the current banking and financial systems will lose the confidence of the people, propelling us downward into a great depression. Politically and economically, a similar environment that resulted historically in the American and French Revolutions is likely to return once again. People here in America may be so outraged, they will demand changes in the government and its purpose and role in our lives, not seen since the Revolutionary War. Both big business and big government will most likely fail to bail us out, and both will be looked upon as having betrayed and deceived the people at large.

Accompanying environmental upheavals will overwhelm many nations and challenge their resources. Just as the colonists rebelled against the English monarchy, the states will rebel against the central government and the giant global corporations. Some states may actually contemplate "seceding" from the Union. Many people will recognize that democracy cannot survive in an ocean of poverty or in a disease-ridden, environmentally degraded world. The transit of Pluto in Capricorn in the mid-1500s coincided with the emergence of Martin Luther and the Protestant Reformation. It may be that people rise to positions of leadership who wish to reform the monopolistic Plutocracy. Like Martin Luther, they may put their manifestos up on the World-Wide Web.

For a time, the state and municipal governments may assume a great deal more responsibility and importance than the federal government. There will be a decentralization of power, putting local governing entities into increasingly important positions. We must remember that the word "responsibility" means "the ability to respond." The extreme weather conditions combined with the great energy crisis will force us to change the way we live at very fundamental levels and only local groups can decide what to do and how to implement it. Mass migrations from newly uninhabitable (Neptune in Pisces) areas may tax the resources of those living in locations that have survived the upheavals.

With Pluto in Capricorn (the established matrices of wealth and power) versus Uranus in Aries (the young and revolutionary), it will remind us of the ancient Chinese curse; "May you live in interesting times." Capricorn symbolizes the elderly, who will likely lose their Social Security, pensions, and healthcare with the collapse of the financial systems that once paid for them. The young people, represented by Aries, may be compelled to take in their parents and their grandparents, while desperately toiling at any kind of work they can get. This will be very difficult since there will likely be extremely high unemployment and the promise of long term gains from investing in the stock market will be a distant memory.

The ultimate outcome may bring about new and more democratic forms of government combined with a return to many of the values of the framers of our constitution. America has a great spirit at its core. This spirit is our legacy. As we pass through this "dark night of the soul," I am of the opinion that we will rise to the historic occasion and rebuild ourselves in such a way to be a model for many other nations of the world. This model will no longer be the greedy, power-mongering economic institutions of the past, but a power-sharing, economically prosperous nation engaging consciously in our own governance. The price we pay for all this will be very high. Many people will lose their lives, others their livelihoods. Those who survive and learn from their history will *not* be doomed to repeat it. They may be the builders of a new kind of democratic capitalism that will usher in an age of prosperity and human potential never before seen in history.

Weapons of Mass Deception

How many of you wish you could go back about a decade and reclaim your retirement accounts and investments you made when you got on the "new economy" bandwagon?

The only consolation you have is that you are not alone. Most of you bought into the notion that, if you invest now, you will have a fortune years later, enough for a comfortable, even luxurious retirement. A fortunate few of you have made a lot of money, surpassing your wildest dreams. Most of you feel seriously disappointed. Pension defaults and poorly invested 401Ks have left you with far less. In order to sustain your standard of living, many of you are burdened with giant mortgages and credit card balances.

We cannot base our future and the future of our grandchildren on mountains of debt, fiat money, and a roulette wheel economy that seems to be rapidly divesting itself from the rule of law. We have become programmed to believe we are a nation of stockholders rather than a nation of innovators, workers and breadwinners. Meanwhile, oil and gas prices are soaring as the reserves are beginning their process of diminishing, as the Middle East is increasingly destabilized by war and ethnic conflict. Our monthly bills for energy, health care, food, and housing are steadily rising. At the time I am writing this book, 48.5 million American people have no health insurance.

It is proudly announced that corporations are now more "productive," increasing profit margins, and that this means we are in the midst of an economic "recovery." Translated, this means that more manufacturing jobs have left the country and, more recently, higher level service jobs in computer systems and engineering and financial services have been transferred out of the U.S.A. In 2002, J.P Morgan-Chase transferred its entire service division to India. Since then, many other sizeable corporations such as Microsoft, IBM and countless others have similar plans. It was recently announced that Haliburton is transferring its primary facility to Dubai.

At first, it may seem that the corporations are helping these nations to develop themselves. What really happens is that they set up a building, hire the people, and within a few years shut down and move to another country where the wages they pay are even lower. Thus, we are presented with increased productivity and rapidly increasing chronic unemployment in higher paying technological areas. Many of the jobs now available are in low-income service areas, frequently paying minimum wage. Now that the real estate bubble is bursting, the jobs added in this sector in recent years are at risk. .

Jeremy Rifkin is the author of *The End of Work: The Decline of the Global Labor Force and the Dawn of the Post-Market Era* and is president of the Foundation on Economic Trends in Washington. He writes in the March 1, 2004 issue of *The Guardian:* "We are losing jobs all over the world. It has reached crisis proportions. In 1995, 800 million were unemployed or underemployed. Today, more than a billion fall into one of these categories." He goes on to say: "As far back as the 1980s, industry analysts were warning that automation would eliminate more and more jobs. Because their forecasts proved some-what premature, the public was lulled into believing that automation was not a problem. Now, however, the software, computer and telecom revolutions, and the proliferation of smart technologies, are finally wreaking havoc on jobs in every country ... Herein lies the conundrum. If dramatic advances in productivity can replace more and more human labor, resulting in more workers being let go from the workforce, where will the consumer demand come from to buy all the potential new products and services? We are being forced to face up to an inherent contradiction at the heart of our market economy that has been present since the very beginning, but is only now becoming irreconcilable."

There have been very few attempts on the part of large banks and corporations to work with employees, offering reduced wages and benefits rather than elimination of jobs. Startlingly, in August 2003, the corporations who laid off the most workers had CEOs who took the biggest pay increases. This trend accelerated in 2004, 2005 and 2006. Not only is the top brass refusing to "share the pain," they are rewarding themselves extensively. The low unemployment figures currently hide the fact that real worker wages are falling, companies are dropping benefits such as healthcare, and many people are forced to work two low-paying jobs.

During this same period, the government was reporting low inflation. I know that my heating bill last winter doubled, my electric bill doubled, my health insurance monthly payment was increased by $119.00, gas for my car went up about $1.50 a gallon, and this is only the beginning. Finally, in 2007, inflation can no longer be denied. It is as obvious as the collective noses on all our faces that the weapons of mass deception had clearly been at work.

America's great journalistic tradition from Ben Franklin and Thomas Paine to Upton Sinclair has been subverted by a mass media frequently interested only in sound-bites and tabloid reporting. We have reason to question whether what we see on television or hear on the radio is reflective of the interests of the corporation who owns the network. Frequently, we have to look at publications outside the U.S.A. for real, comprehensive news. We are just beginning to wake up. As I write this book, I am seeing a few in the media apologizing for the past and attempting to resurrect a code of more truthful and thorough reporting.

People are just beginning to face the fact that huge federal expenditures on military engagements combined with the tax breaks for the upper five percent in income are threatening the infrastructure of highway systems, teachers, police and fire fighters because of shrinking budgets. Federal budget deficits and higher energy costs will ultimately cause interest rates to rise, with or without Alan Greenspan or Ben Bernanke. The Great Depression of the 1930s, in part, was caused by the collapse of the British pound sterling that was then, like the dollar now, the global currency. The frenzied buying "on margin" in the stock market and our inability to back up our banking system, led to the systemic collapse. All these factors are lining up before our eyes today. The global derivatives trade referred to in previous chapters has skyrocketed to a notional value of around $370 trillion and the proliferation of hedge funds throughout the world have set us up in a speculative roulette wheel economy that could easily "fall off the cliff." (See Appendix F for astrological chart of the NYSE.)

The Astrological Chart of the Federal Reserve

The natal horoscope of the Federal Reserve was put into place when Pres. Woodrow Wilson signed the Glass-Owen Bill on December 23, 1913 at 6:02 PM in Washington. D.C. (See Appendix G for astrological chart of the FRB.) The great economic catastrophe for America in the 20ᵗʰ century was the stock market crash of October 1929. Transiting Pluto (the planet symbolizing crisis, catastrophe and big money) hit the rising Mars in this chart at that time. This Mars is located on the south node of Pluto. Between 1931 and 1932, Pluto was square transiting Uranus in Aries, opposing Jupiter (expansion) in Capricorn in the 7ᵗʰ House (legal partnerships) in this chart, forming a devastating Cardinal T-square. The Great Depression was underway in the U.S., fascism and militarism proliferated in Germany, Italy and Japan, while the Communist dictatorship in Russia ruthlessly imposed its will on its people.

In the period 2008 – 2017, transiting Pluto in Capricorn will begin a series of destabilizing aspects similar to that period and will once again make squares with transiting Uranus in

Aries between 2010 – 2016. It is my prediction that by 2017 – 2018, as transiting Pluto opposes the Federal Reserve Mars and its own south node, the Federal Reserve institution, as we now know it, will no longer exist. Either something else will replace it, or nothing will replace it, but this cartel of global banks as it currently exists, connected to our government and financial systems, will likely come to an end.

It is now time for us to prepare ourselves to live in a very different world, and examine alternatives to the present system that is on a course from self-deception to self-destruction. We must move beyond the economic and social frameworks that promote concentrations of power into the hands of multinational corporations who either overthrow or buy out governments to further their own narrow purposes and agendas. We must eliminate war as an option, along with the development of arsenals of catastrophic weaponry.

Beyond all this is a core spirit of freedom and self-determination that has brought the people of this nation back from the brink over and over again.

The Quiet Revolution – Moving into the Solution

Increasing numbers of people in this country and abroad are opting out of the mainstream, taking buyouts, cashing in their chips, leaving their corporate jobs, paying off their debt and selling their houses in the suburbs. These people are not hippies from the 1960s or angry revolutionaries plotting attacks on the government. They abide by the law, pay their taxes, love their children, appreciate their friends, and even take care of their parents.

Many have already formed what could be called "intentional communities" or co-housing neighborhoods, consisting of solar houses designed for maximum energy efficiency, communal organic farms and gardens, community meeting houses designed for childcare, and dining, and shared computer facilities. Although individual housing is privately owned, the land ownership is shared and the people who live there share in the gardening and maintenance. These communities are distinguished from religious communes in that you can be a member who is of any religious faith or ethnic background. Since there is no hierarchy, they are democratically governed by consensus, and all decisions are voted upon by all residents. There is great support for diversity of background racially, ethnically and economically. Some people there are self-employed, others have outside jobs. Some people are retired, others are stay-at-home parents. They share ideas, and help each other in times of need. They feel their children are safe and are growing up in an environment of attentive, caring adults. Their elders are receiving the care they need, while being active and valued participants. They are, quite simply, reviving the spirit of community in a new way.

I recommend *Eco-Village of Ithaca* by Liz Walker (New Society Publishers) about the founding and hard-won success of this co-housing community in Ithaca, N.Y., located next to both Ithaca College and Cornell University. Her heart-felt story reflects a passion to discover and create a pathway to a sustainable, renewable and harmonious way of living that may restore to us an authentic joy in life itself. Here is an example of people who have chosen to be part of the "solution."

There will be new groups of "think tanks," populist organizations, and democratic "grass roots" societies meeting locally and communicating over the Internet; all dedicated to coming up with innovative ideas and creative solutions to the serious problems ahead.

Preparing for the Inevitable

In addition, as we approach the threshold of exhaustion of oil and gas deposits throughout the world, we will have to face the possibility that our electrical "grid" will be threatened with a shutdown. Oil and gas prices will likely skyrocket beyond our ability to pay. Although it will certainly not replace oil and gas, solar housing and technology, combined with the use of windmills may ensure a significant *reduction of dependency* on fossil fuels and avert catastrophe. If structural unemployment is becoming a reality, and we have every reason to believe it is, we need a micro-economy that could sustain us through these times without most of us falling into abject poverty.

Dr. Jeremy Leggett, Chief Executive of Solarcentury and a member of the UK's Renewables Advisory Board, reports in the June 19, 2004 Issue of *The Guardian:* "By mixing and matching renewable technologies, any aspect of modern life could be powered reliably by renewables. All we need is imagination, the will governments usually reserve for waging war, the leadership from responsible companies and time to make the switch."

The astrological configurations are issuing a warning that we have very little time left. Indeed, the time to mobilize our resources for the future is now! It is important that alliances between governments and industry, such as those in times of war, be inspired to a quality of innovation and collective resolve we have seldom seen in modern history.

A Shining Example

An example of someone truly prepared for the future is one of my forward-looking clients, who opted out of mainstream suburbia by buying a farm in Pennsylvania. She has renovated the house, guest cottage and the barn, is boarding horses, renting the cottage and creating an organic garden. She has made friends with her neighbors, some of whom are her contractors, and she is in awe at their skills and willingness to tackle projects. Next year, she is planning to investigate the use of solar panels, a generator, and a windmill, striving for clean energy efficiency and independence. A successful entrepreneur, the head of a placement company, she has been able to finance her farm. Soon, it will pay for itself. She tells me she has never been so happy and invigorated. Her children have fallen in love with the place and are learning skills they would never be exposed to in school. When my husband and I visited her, I noticed how relaxed, enthusiastic and optimistic she was. Most of all, her neighbors and friends were always "dropping in" and there was a warmth and fellowship there that is a distant memory to many people today.

Many people are being worked to exhaustion in jobs that no longer have meaning, and long to create new lives for themselves. Others are jobless, going bankrupt and see no future for themselves within the current economic and social framework. Many of us want more time to spend with our families and those nearest and dearest to us. Everyone wants to have time to enjoy the forests (fast disappearing), the oceans (rapidly rising), and the open land (rapidly disappearing). This is the beginning of a discontent that will bring about the kind and quality of change that can transform us, enlighten us, and save us.

The "Versus" Society

Many people in America have noticed over the past twenty years the growth of a litigious, defensive, adversarial culture that has gotten out of hand. This has come at the expense of the society itself. Doctors versus insurance companies versus patients; parents versus teachers versus children; the corporation versus corporate employees; wives versus husbands versus lawyers, et al.

I do not believe for one moment that we should revoke our right to sue wrongdoers. The ordinary individuals have to have legal recourse to protect their rights from cheaters and more powerful institutions. But the civil court system is simply overwhelmed so much that it has serious difficulty enforcing its own decisions. This incredibly angry attitude we have developed toward each other is a fast ticket to a societal nervous breakdown.

There are people with greater expertise and knowledge than I who have been unable to effectively change the system or stop this tidal wave. Meanwhile, lawyers and insurance companies are the beneficiaries. Medical malpractice insurance has skyrocketed through the stratosphere with many doctors forced to pay out over $100,000 per year in insurance premiums. A startling number of doctors are leaving their specialties because of the high cost of these premiums.

High-end lawyers are benefiting from divorces involving large estates and bitter hatreds. Corporations are now getting employees from other nations rather than pay high wages to Americans, whose union organizers may have priced them out of the job market. What happened to the notion of working together, taking pay cuts rather than losing jobs? The "versus" society is inflicting itself with wounds that may be fatal if it cannot stop the insanity.

The "With You" Society

There is an old notion that may be revolutionary in a culture that values gladiatorial competition, the accumulation of personal wealth at any cost, and a kind of insulated privacy and unaccountability that protects people from the consequences of their actions.

This old, grandmotherly notion is that we are all here *with* each other, with the earth, its climate and the life it has given us, with other nations, with other religions, with people we like, with people we don't like, and most of all, with people we don't know. History has shown us over and over again that widely experienced poverty spreads disease, crime, terror and war. Recent history is showing us that greenhouse gases are altering the earth's climate and industrial toxins take an immeasurable toll on all life. The fact is that we are here *with* poverty, terror, and global warming.

We all heard in 2000 that the human population on earth went over the 6 billion mark. Our modern media technologies enable us to glimpse into the lives of people in failed societies, living in dire poverty. The destruction of the rain forests threatens to create deserts where there once was life. We can see the melting Matterhorn, the breakup of the glaciers at the South Pole, the extreme climate changes throughout the world. We would rather change the dial to sexy dramas, tabloid shouting matches, and "reality" shows to escape these realities after a long hard day at work. It is simply too much to comprehend. It is down right depressing to see it, hear it, and most of all, to feel it. But we cannot get around the fact that it is happening.

The Promise of Aquarius

In the next twenty-year period, we will be moving from the "versus" society to the "with you" society, not because we initially want to do it, but because we have to do it. The crises that lie ahead of us will awaken us on some fundamental level to work *with* each other to innovate and create new ways of life, new micro- and macro-economic systems that sustain a healthy environment, a system of international law to protect the rights of workers, protect an industry's inventions and toll positions, and insure human rights. But all of this is hopeless idealism without a collective consciousness shift that will consist of the understanding that we are all in this together.

My Prophecy:

The Worst Case Scenario

The upcoming transit of Pluto in Capricorn (2008 – 2024) took place previously at the time of the Protestant Reformation in Europe that led to the Thirty-Years War. Most recently, it occurred at the time of the American Revolution followed by the French Revolution and the historic rise of democracy. The results were great and bloody conflicts that overthrew the prevailing established empires, religions and governments. Many people died in wars and systemic collapses. At the same time, great ideas took hold. The notions of religious freedom, free market capitalism, and democracy began to manifest in human history.

Uranus will transit the sign of Aries May 2010 – March 2019. Previous transits of Uranus in Aries have coincided with cycles of economic depressions, the most recent one having taken place from 1927 – 1935. From December 2012 – March

2015, Uranus is square (in conflict with) Pluto, symbolizing the breakdown of prevailing governmental structures, a collapse of banking and financial systems, and the possibility of armed revolutionaries storming the gates of capitol cities.

In the 1930s, many people thought capitalism and democracy were abject failures; thus the rise of fascism in Germany and Italy, and Stalinism in Communist Russia. Many intellectuals here in the United States regrettably joined the Communist Party as a backlash to the greedy and powerful capitalists whose policies and practices they saw as the cause of the economic collapse.

Later on, in the 1940s and 1950s, these people became the objects of the McCarthy era Communist witch-hunts, the consequence of Cold War paranoia. By then, the U.S. economy was flourishing and we went on to invest in public education, highway systems and an infrastructure enabling America to become the most prosperous nation on earth. Most people today have forgotten the tragedy, disillusionment and consequences of the Great Depression. They have taken for granted the profound investment our society made in its people afterwards.

The worst case scenario is that we will have to repeat the collapse and suffering; that the present generation, having little if any interest in history, will have to endure another systemic failure. Most people will be in total shock and have no preparation whatsoever for a society collapsing under a mountain of governmental, corporate, and personal debt.

Insurance companies may go bankrupt due to the destruction of property as the result of severe climatic changes and extreme weather. Just as the Baby Boomers will be retiring, our national debt may be such that Social Security and Medicare may effectively come to an end, pension funds (many of which are already under-funded) may end, and millions of elderly and disabled people may descend into poverty.

Already, foreclosures, bankruptcies, poverty and homelessness and violent crime are increasing throughout our nation. In the meantime, the television news tells us our economy is "booming," and the weapons of mass deception are effectively anesthetizing us as we fall asleep on the couch after a ten-hour workday, exhausted while watching the evening news.

We may witness wars between nations over the remaining oil and gas reserves in a desperate last attempt to prop up their energy grids. Those who have replaced fossil fuels with other technologies will truly be the survivors who will live to tell the tale!

We will likely be experiencing profound disillusionment with the federal government in Washington. There may emerge a movement toward a *decentralization* of power, increasing the governance and importance of the states and local communities. With frequently cataclysmic climate changes, local governments and communities will have to address their needs in different ways. However, the people in power won't give up their positions easily just as the aristocracies did not easily give way in the 18ᵗʰ century. There is an effort being made at this time to create a "new world order" contained within the notion of combining Canada, the U.S. and Mexico economically in such a way that these nations would lose their sovereignty. Instead, the multi-national giant corporations would circumvent laws and regulations since they would not be held accountable by the governments of the nations. Environmental laws, labor laws and protection of human rights would likely be a thing of the past. The rule of the "people" would effectively end, enabling the ruling elites to abolish the democratic process, and use the police force to suppress demonstrators and dissenters. This scenario, indeed, would give birth to a second American Revolution.

Because Pluto was in Capricorn at the time of the American Revolution, I think we may form new "continental congresses," claiming autonomy for ourselves closer to home. If the central government has lost its credibility, having sold out to the robber barons, states are not likely to want to pay taxes to support it. They will want to support their own local tax and infrastructures. Remember the cry of the revolutionaries: "No taxation without representation!"

There is a possibility this may be the beginning of the end for the United States as we presently know it. As we go into the 2020s, regional differences may cause states to want to secede from the Union. I am of the opinion that we will, as before, be able to survive this crisis intact as a nation, but not without extreme effort. Ironically, at the same time, there will be the beginnings of a World Government and rule of law encompassing economies, the environment, and a global police force to settle regional conflicts and prevent war. By that time, the United Nations may have either dissolved or reinvented itself into a more effective world governing entity.

Energy and the Environment

In 2012 – 2014, Pluto is in a degree (8-9 degrees Capricorn) that has been historically associated with earthquakes of significant magnitude, especially in California. Uranus transited this degree in 1906 and again in 1989, when we saw powerful earthquakes hit San Francisco. The square of this degree to Uranus in Aries symbolically magnifies the cycle. In addition, as Saturn, Neptune, and Uranus all passed through this degree in 1989 through 1994, a large volcano erupted in the Philippines, altering the global climate for several years. These configurations also are notable in the horoscopes of the U.S., the UK, China, Japan, Russia, the Czech Republic, Iran, Indonesia, the Philippines, Mexico and Peru, suggesting earth and climate changes accompanied by crises related to their leadership.

Capricorn is a sign associated with real and lasting consequences. If nations alter their present course and face up to what needs to be done, signing and implementing environmental agreements, ending the dominance of fossil fuel industries, many of these configurations will play out in a more modest way. If not, global warming, glaciers melting, and pollution escalating will truly take their toll, making it impossible for populations to survive in many locations. Severe drought due to the loss of mountain glaciers will hit many parts of the world, including the Middle East, Africa, China, India and parts of the western United States, while others in coastal regions will suffer inundations of ocean waters. Fresh water will become more precious than oil. As Neptune enters the sign of Pisces in 2011, millions of refugees will leave their uninhabitable lands, overwhelming the resources of the nations whose borders they cross.

In August 2010, a highly challenging configuration of Mars, Saturn, Jupiter, Uranus and Pluto suggests, as I have stated in previous chapters, we will essentially run out of access to oil and money, generating a great crisis of leadership in the U.S.A. and many other nations. There will likely be significant wars over the remaining territories that contain the last reserves. In his book *The Long Emergency* (Atlantic Monthly Press, New York), James Howard Kunstler writes about a desperate fight for survival in a world running out of energy reserves. He points out that the problem resides in the ratio of how much energy we have to use to mine the energy we need. This is referred to as EroEI. As we are forced to dig deeper into the oceans and into the remaining deposits on the land, the cost and usage of energy to reach these reserves will eventually exceed what we gain. His vision for the future includes societal destruction throughout our present civilization, plunging us backward into a pre-industrial world.

In addition, global climate change will make the burning of fossil fuels increasingly dangerous to all life on earth. It is now thought that previous extinctions of life on earth are re-lated to warming of ocean waters, releasing carbon dioxide into the atmosphere and depleting oxygen in water and air.

Energy prices will initially skyrocket and overwhelm most people's ability to pay. In addition to the unquenchable thirst for oil in the U.S.A. and Europe, the nations of China and India with their huge populations will increase their demand for the black gold. The possibility that oil wars could break out throughout the world will be increased.(See Appendix H for a natal chart of China, and Appendix I for India.)

In the last analysis, the need for energy to maintain our very civilization will force us to discover or invent new sources or approach an "energy Armageddon."

Best Case Scenario

We will step up to the plate now, while we still have the economic resources to do something about what is to come. We will develop windmill and solar technologies, develop battery technology, and focus with great resolve on energy use reduction. With enough financial investment and resolve, our scientists and engineers will discover an entirely new way to generate a form of energy that is inexhaustible. We will end the political domination of the oil companies and encourage these very corporations to go into the non-fossil fuel energy business. We may even create healthy industries based on new energy technology, providing jobs and encouraging innovation. There will no longer be a need for our government to be involved in shady and dangerous alliances with nations in the Middle East.

We will come to a realization that globalism is an attempt to throw an ideological veil over the financial interests of an emerging class of trans-national capitalists; that it has created optimal conditions for the unrestricted exercise of greed and that it is *not* a structural part of the capitalist system. We will recognize the need to return to the entrepreneurial climate of smaller companies and invent our way out of the crises.

Our government will, hopefully, have the will to exit its devastating and expensive occupation of Iraq, pay down our giant budget deficits, get rid of tax breaks for the upper five percent of the nation, and realistically prepare our nation for the crises to come. We will recognize the need to create democratically governed communities and local economies that can survive and prosper during the times ahead with local organic farms, solar houses and buildings, and most of all, a spirit of willingness to help and support each other.

We need to encourage the entrepreneurial spirit that has always been at the heart of America, with tax breaks and subsidies for new inventions and industries that will solve our problems.

The truth is that the giant monopolistic corporations rarely produce the quality of innovation that comes from individual inventors and entrepreneurs. Instead, they "buy out" the creative small business for its product and its customer base.

Once they become "big," the encouraging, creative atmosphere frequently disappears.

What really lends hope to this otherwise bleak landscape, however, are the presences of extremely wealthy and successful individuals who really care about a better tomorrow and are willing to invest hundreds of millions of dollars in campaigns, programs and charities designed to improve the lot of other human beings. Richard Branson has offered millions of dollars to persons who invent a new source of energy. Another agency is the Bill and Melinda Gates Foundation, the largest charitable organization in the world, recently contributed to by billionaire Warren Buffet. Oprah Winfrey has contributed millions to schools and organizations she has founded to offer opportunities for many who would otherwise be consigned to lives of hardship and poverty. Al Gore and Robert Redford have set up organizations to reverse environmentally destructive trends. These genuinely altruistic people may be an important component in rescuing us from a more terrible fate. Largely, however, it will be all of us working together who have the real power to decide our collective fate. Humanity must fundamentally change the way it lives, with the tools of intelligence, compassion and innovation.

Neptune currently moving through Aquarius (1998 – 2012) is symbolic of friendship, shared information, respect for individuality amidst a spirit of cooperation. It is a sign that possesses hope and optimism, even in the darkest hours. It is a sign of genius and innovation that can open entirely new passageways to the future, whether through technology or through a kind of generalized faith in the human spirit. It embodies the true spirit of the entrepreneur, the explorer, the inventor, the humanitarian.

Will our civilization have to journey to the edge of annihilation or will we discover, out of our tribulation, a new genesis, a concept of life and love that unites us on our pilgrimage together on the planet. Instead of violating nature, will we work in concert with life on earth? Will we integrate science and technology, political and economic systems in such a way that benefits all living creatures? Will we see ourselves as part of a great, living, evolving system with the capability to inspire itself to reach beyond its own limitations?

Our children are watching, listening, and waiting to experience the legacy they will inherit. Can we look away?

New Frameworks of Consciousness

For thousands of years, religious mythologies explained human behavior and framed our experiences for us, making some kind of sense out of the chaos of life, keeping fear at bay. In the 19th and 20th centuries, science and technology influenced us to look at ourselves from a different perspective. We needed to study ourselves "under the microscope" in the laboratory, seeing ourselves as biological machines whose functioning could be dissected and measured. A new subject emerged to express this need. It was modern psychology.

Interestingly, at the beginning of this era, Mary Shelly wrote *Frankenstein*, whose warnings still resonate in our lives today. Beware of piecing dead physical parts together, turning on the electricity, and calling it a human being.

James, Freud, Jung, Adler, Skinner are names out of our history books; fathers and framers of the modern psychological movement. Certainly many of us have studied the experimental data, statistics, and observations made about what makes us do what we do, think what we think, feel what we feel.

A great many of us have attempted to improve our lives with some form of psychotherapy. Many people today are following the most recent trends and are taking antidepressants, neural relaxants, or hormonal replacements to fix our feelings and responses and help us to function as we believe we should. And this society demands that we function consistently in the workplace, the marketplace, the home front, like a well-oiled machine.

The fact is, religion and psychology are fields of great complexity and contain within them subtle differentiations, as well as complex evolutionary processes. But I believe they are actually in their infancy in the sense that something else is about to be born that lifts us out of blind superstition and/or cold mechanical reductionism. The last two transits of Pluto in Capricorn sowed the seeds of religious freedom and the concept of a democratic government by and for the people. This transit may usher in new concepts of social governance leading to entirely new ways of life.

My prophecy is that humanity is poised at the threshold of the cave, looking at the frightful demons we must slay before we can leave the agonizing darkness. We must leave the ancient tribal fears and hatreds that divide us into warring cultures. Competition for territory and resources that have led to mass extinctions in the past must give way to a truly mature sensibility of cooperation and self-control for the greater good. Like the many prophets before me, I am also imbued with the sense that we will emerge into a new set of frameworks of consciousness that reach beyond all our imaginings.

Chapter 5

Prophecies for Our Children and Grandchildren in America

Jupiter Conjunct Saturn in Aquarius (December 2020)

A Look into the Distance

The children born between 1980 and 2000 (both markers for the last two conjunctions of Jupiter to Saturn – see Appendix J) will be between the ages of 20 to 40 years when Jupiter conjuncts Saturn in the sign of Aquarius in December 2020 (see Appendix K). This astrological configuration of Jupiter (expansion) conjunct Saturn (contraction) is historically associated with philosophical and political changes. This generation will have survived great challenges for which their society was likely unprepared. They are, fortunately, an amazingly strong generation. The ones born between 1983 and 1995 have Pluto in Scorpio, the sign of death and rebirth. Those born in 1993 have the great conjunction of Neptune to Uranus in Capricorn and the square of Pluto in Scorpio to Saturn in Aquarius, coinciding with development of the Internet, the Industrial Revolution in China and the signing of NAFTA Treaty with all of its promise and disappointment.

They will have grown up with the Internet, cell phones, biogenetic engineering, photographs of the surface of Mars, and antidepressants. Over half of them will have parents who are divorced and be in "blended families." They will have moved around more frequently than other generations before them. They will remember great economic prosperity and a systemic collapse of that prosperity into an environment of upheaval and change. First, they had everything and then they had nothing, then the dawning of something else.

Where their parents were speculative, these children will be cautious. Where their parents lived in a world that valued hyper-competitive individualism, these children will value working creatively as individuals in teams and groups. The environmental mess left behind by previous generations will be theirs to clean up and they will most assuredly take on this monumental task.

In the Age of Aquarius, the challenge will be to express a belief in the freedom and uniqueness of the individual that operates in concert with the well-being of the society as a whole. Its opposite sign, Leo, is the symbol of the cult of personality, the hero myth, the movie star, at its worst, the dictator. Aquarius must work with Leo in a kind of balance between the people-at-large and its charismatic leaders. Creativity and inventiveness must be encouraged. Individuality must be honored. A renewed desire to be of service to humanity must be restored.

At the same time, we will begin to see ourselves as part of great evolving systems; the ecological environment of the earth, the societal transformations of human history, the flow of technological innovation that has given birth to human progress through the ages.

One of my teenaged grandchildren surprised me recently with his insight that, although historic apocalypses were indeed tragic and terrible, they have always resulted in the rebirth of civilization into something vastly better. One of my much younger grandchildren recently said to me he thinks God might look something like the Statue of Liberty! Are these the children of Aquarius?

The Age of Energy and the Green Revolution

From Benjamin Franklin's discovery of electricity to Thomas Edison's harnessing of it, modern times came into being with the creation of energy and the dawn of the electric age. This was followed by the nuclear age and all its frightening potential. Whatever the energy source, civilization as we know it today would be absolutely nonexistent without it. Whether in autos or in cell phones, battery technology will take on increasing importance. The mandate will be how to supply energy without fossil fuel and its devastating effect on the environment. A new series of breakthroughs will be made out of absolute necessity; solar power, windmill power, and something else we have not yet discovered.

Our grandchildren will live to see an age when energy will be abundantly available without the use of fossil fuels. Battery technology will be perfected and the wireless revolution will be complete. But the toll already taken on the planet by greenhouse warming, chemical and nuclear contamination and the ensuing climatic changes will be immeasurable. They will have to survive this. The devastating effects of dramatic climate changes will likely reduce human population across the face of the earth. The survivors will have carefully crafted communities using new scientific technologies yet to be conceived.

A substantial economy built around decontamination and environmental cleanup will likely be our grandchildren's inheritance.

Population Reduction

Ever since humankind has walked the earth, we have been invested with the passion to bring forth children and populate the planet. There will come a time of such great difficulty that many people will not want to bring children into a world of poverty and seeming hopelessness. The transformation of land masses, the destabilization of climates, and the breakdown of economies means the loss of health care and many of the diseases that have been contained may kill millions of people, especially in developing nations. The elderly may find life difficult, if not impossible to endure. With their economic and medical support systems gone, many will perish in poverty.

Especially hard hit will be the developing nations who already lack the infrastructure and resources to save themselves. Some nations will suffer such severe environmental destruction that they will have to leave their shores in mass migrations. Other nations will lack the resources to accommodate the immigrants and many will be overwhelmed by these people and try to turn them away. This period will be the "dark night of the soul" for humanity in modern times.

The Survivors

Our children and grandchildren will be the ones who will have to overcome these hardships, transcend despair, and rise above it all to a new level of consciousness. Those who inhabit a place of hope and light at the center of their being will be the survivors and creators of a new habitation on earth. Instead of being plunderers, they will be caretakers. Instead of being destroyers, they will be creators. They will rescue us from the tragic failure of the human experiment. *They will be witnesses to a rebirth of life on earth within an entirely new context.*

Those who survive to create this new civilization will have learned the lessons of history and will cherish the biological diversity on earth, operating cooperatively within its miraculous system. These children of tomorrow will likely travel to other planets and may even peer into different dimensions that are today's hypothesis and tomorrow's reality. They will likely develop a practice of medicine we can hardly conceive of today; engineering a new human form free of diseases common now and with a life expectancy far longer. To them, our present civilization will seem harsh, selfish and shortsighted.

For years, we have read the science fiction novels and seen the movies that deal with all the technological marvels of the future, but nearly always circumscribed by the primitive, violent warlike stupidity of the past. What is missing is the most important ingredient; social and spiritual evolution beyond the "warring tribes" model of governance.

It is my prophecy that we will *not* take this evil into our future with us, because it will simply not survive the profound changes here on earth that lie ahead. It is as if something is pushing us toward the next evolutionary stage of human existence. I am reminded of a saying by Carlos Castaneda:

"We either make ourselves miserable, or we make ourselves strong. The amount of work is the same."

Chapter 6

Sedna - A Planet of the 21st Century

The End and the Beginning

As I write this book, a new planet has been discovered with its orbit in the outer reaches of our solar system, beyond Pluto. This is extremely exciting to astrologers since planetary discoveries for each century for the past 300 years have symbolized breakthroughs in consciousness and progress for humanity at an unprecedented rate.

Now that we have the technology, we are able to observe new planets, asteroids, and still unclassified heavenly bodies. Recently, astronomers (amidst great conflict among themselves) pronounced Pluto to be a "dwarf planet" and the previously designated asteroid Ceres to be also a "dwarf planet."

In the 18th century, Uranus (innovation, electricity, democracy) was discovered, coinciding with the American and French revolutions, the advent of democracy, the discovery of electricity and the ascendancy of science. In the 19th century, Neptune (vision and illusion, liquids and chemicals) was discovered, coinciding with the discovery of oil, the Industrial Revolution, Darwin's Theory of Evolution, the birth of communism and the beginning of modern medicine. In the 20th century, Pluto (creation and destruction of wealth, power, and life) was discovered, coinciding with quantum physics, two world wars, the invention of nuclear weapons, space travel, the advent of computers, and the rise of the capitalistic "plutocracy."

All of our planets, up to now, have been named after Greco-Roman gods and goddesses with their attendant insights into human archetypal behavior and mythic historic themes. This particular name chosen by astronomers in 2004 is a definite departure from the past. Her name is Sedna, taken from a fable handed down from the Inuit peoples of Alaska.

Significantly improved telescopes and technologies have enabled us to discover Sedna, along with surveying a whole new group of planetary bodies orbiting out beyond Pluto in the area named the Kuiper Belt. Very recently, another body was discovered and named Eris.

Because Sedna has been discovered and named so recently, little has been written about it in the astrological community. The most extensive and comprehensive article I have located was in the August/September issue of *The Mountain Astrologer,* titled: "Out on the Edge with Sedna," by astrologer Bryan Trussler.

Sedna is the central figure in an Alaskan Inuit legend with an interesting story that has resonance with many of the issues of our time. She was a princess, the daughter of a tribal ruler, and said to be beautiful, vain and very particular about men. This led her to refuse to marry any of the suitors presented to her by her father. While Sedna was in a boat on a fishing trip with her father and several of his men, a storm broke out. A great "demon bird" came after Sedna to make her his wife, circling the boat, casting an evil shadow. In all the fright and confusion, she fell into the sea. Her father made the decision that it was too dangerous to try to save her and headed for the shore. She screamed and tried to grab the side of the boat, losing her fingers in the process as the men on the boat severed them with their oars. Finally, she sank to the bottom of the ocean and settled there. Her fingers were said to have developed into sea creatures and her screams and cries are said to be heard to this day, whenever a great storm howls across the ocean.

Sedna was recently discovered while in Taurus, a sign traditionally associated with the earth and all its teeming multitudes of life. In August 2005 – February 2006, transiting Mars (aggression) in Taurus went over Sedna, square transiting Neptune (the ocean). During that period, hurricanes Katrina, Rita and Wilma devastated the Gulf Coast of the U.S.A., and a serious cyclone swept over Japan. Between June 25 – August 7, 2007, Mars will transit Taurus again, over the same configuration.

I believe Sedna is falling overboard into the rising ocean and is crying for help. Are we ignoring her cries? Are our land-masses disappearing, covered by an angry, stormy sea? As the polar glaciers are melting and breaking up, are many species of life awaiting their deaths while we refuse to listen?

I can only venture a guess as to what this great discovery will mean. I would very much like to believe that, with her discovery, we will restore the life threatened with extinction on earth and in the waters of the ocean; that we will evolve into being loving caretakers of life on our planet. Being a feminine archetype, Sedna may (along with the current transit of Uranus in Pisces) coincide with an awakening in our collective spirit of the need to experience life on earth as cherished and sacred rather than something to be conquered and degraded. We may also see the rise of "outraged women" to prominence in government and in the media, who will contribute to the environmental movement, the protection of the family, and peacemaking. This may be wishful thinking on my part, for Sedna, in the legend, preferred to remain unmarried and childless. Her own father and his companions were responsible for her death since they did not rescue her. At the bottom of the sea, she expresses her anger through violent storms. Could we all fear the wrath of the abused woman, the altered seas, the endangered life on earth?

Ironically, Alaska, the home of the Inuit peoples, is experiencing the melting of the permafrost and the destruction of many of the eco-systems of the native tribes. It is estimated that these people have resided in their locations for about 2,000 years, roughly corresponding with the Age of Pisces. As the glaciers melt, much of the land mass may return to the sea and change the landscape for thousands of years to come.

It is my sincere hope that the princess may generously hand our very own lives back to us as we put the ancient, obsolete and destructive patterns of the old civilization behind us. I think as Sedna speaks to us through weather extremes and stormy seas, we should listen. Our answer to her cries may change the "tide" of history in a monumental effort to rescue the environment and preserve life on earth.

The looming question is: Will we want to extend our hands out to her and pull her to safety? On the other hand, it is possible she may be a symbol of primal self-absorption, an inability to see beyond one's immediate needs and pleasures; and a total disregard for caring for the welfare of one's society or culture in a larger sense.

The storms, earthquakes, tsunamis are her messages to us that we must elevate human consciousness to a new evolutionary level in which we reach out our arms to her in spite of her disregard for us, pull her out of her watery grave, and in choosing to forgive her, rescue ourselves so that we may live to see a new rising of the sun.

Index of Signs and Planets Pertaining to Historic Cycles

Aries - Cardinal Fire. Ruling Planet - Mars

Pioneers, aspires, energizes, invents, rebels to insure the rights of the individual. An Aries cycle begins everything anew after the destruction of the old systems. It represents war and armaments or new inventions; social rebellions or the introduction of new societal concepts.

Taurus - Fixed Earth. Ruling Planet - Venus

Builds, constructs, secures, finances, owns. A Taurus cycle secures ownership of real estate either through conquest or purchase, decides national boundaries, repairs infrastructure through civil engineering or building construction, and determines the distribution of wealth.

Gemini - Mutable Air. Ruling Planet - Mercury

Grasps and communicates ideas, develops language skills and locomotion, educates children and socially interacts with relatives and neighbors. A Gemini cycle emphasizes mass educational projects, new modes of travel, the press, clever inventions, and competition (sibling rivalry) for attention.

Cancer - Cardinal Water. Ruling Planet (satellite) - The Moon

Develops feeling and intuition to ensure comfort and survival, is concerned with food and medicine, nurtures and feeds the young, secures fundamental cultural values in families and nations. A Cancerian cycle reveres history and tradition, is patriotic, nationalistic, and frequently retreats into defending the nation against outsiders.

Leo - Fixed Fire. Ruling Planet (star) - The Sun

Promotes dramatic self-expression, creativity and entrepreneurship, reveres children, supports leadership skills, sports, and the media arts. A Leo cycle challenges leaders in governments and industries to rise or fall based on their charisma, showmanship, and their ability to inspire others. The dangers that are present lie in movements toward dictatorship.

Virgo - Mutable Earth. Ruling Planet - Mercury

Is concerned with perfecting skills in the job market, the rights of workers, health and human services, and the military service. A Virgo cycle frequently reflects difficulties and challenges related to employment or unemployment and the need for corporate efficiency and productivity. Sanitation, hygiene, and civil improvements in the quality of life are major concerns.

Libra - Cardinal Air. Ruling Planet - Venus

Creates balance and diplomacy among individuals and nations, works toward equality of opportunity for all, and negotiates peace agreements. A Libra cycle attempts to settle disputes and stop wars and is therefore often accused of indecision and slowing up of the process. This cycle is usually led by idealists and is famous for peaceful protest movements.

Scorpio - Fixed Water. Ruling Planet - Pluto

Intensifies, concentrates, and confronts the crises born of the use and misuse of power. It has rulership over volcanoes and earth changes and nuclear confrontations when combined with planetary tensions. A Scorpio cycle often decides who controls the collective financial resources of a nation and whether it is used for destructive or constructive purposes, thereby bringing about explosive confrontation among various contenders for this control.

Sagittarius - Mutable Fire. Ruling Planet - Jupiter

Expands economies and civilizations throughout the globe, through travel, trade, and information technologies. A Sagittarius cycle is one of unbridled optimism, continuing to borrow, speculate, and explore until it simply runs out of funds or has consumed all its resources. It will resort to war in order to continue its expansionary efforts and eventually exhausts the treasury bringing the cycle to a halt.

Capricorn - Cardinal Earth. Ruling Planet - Saturn

Contracts, limits, and defines national policies, often corresponding with economic recessions or depressions, and forces a "changing of the guard" in both economic and state governance. Frequently, the old power structures fail and fall, giving new people a chance to step up to the plate and take on the heavy responsibilities of devising an entirely new order with a vision that extends over the long term.

Aquarius - Fixed Air. Ruling Planet - Uranus

Invents, transforms and organizes groups to participate in technological breakthroughs, social experiments, and new ideas. Aquarius is the sign behind the concept of democracy, liberty, freedom and intellectual enlightenment. It is associated with the discovery and harnessing of electricity. This cycle usually brings forth scientific discoveries that effects the masses of people for generations to come.

Pisces - Mutable Water. Ruling Planet - Neptune

Dissolves previously held convictions and beliefs about life, yearns for a journey to other worlds and states of consciousness through travel over the ocean to new adventures or "trips" that result from the use of substances such as drugs or alcohol. It symbolizes liquids, thus bringing up issues over water (flooding), oil and chemicals. A Pisces cycle can produce geniuses or religious fanatics, great artists, musicians and filmmakers or suicidal drug addicts. More than anything, this cycle seeks to express what lends a greater meaning to life beyond ordinary existence.

Bibliography

Books:

Encyclopedia of Astrology, by Nicholas deVore, Philosophical Library New York, Bonanza Books, Div. of Crown Publishers, Inc. New York, NY. 1947

The Book of World Horoscopes by Nicholas Campion (second printing revised 1996), Cinnabar Books, Bristol, UK

Horoscope for the New Millennium by E. Alan Meece, Llewellyn Publications, St. Paul, MN, 1997

Perfectly Legal by David Cay Johnston, Penguin Group, New York, NY, 2003

The Long Emergency by James Howard Kunstler, Grove/Atlantic, Inc., New York, NY, 2005

Confessions of an Economic Hit Man by John Perkins, Plume, Published by Penguin Group, New York, NY, 2006

Nemesis: The Last Days of the American Republic by Chalmers Johnson, Metropolitan Books, Henry Holt and Company, LLC, New York, NY, 2006

Eco Village at Ithaca by Liz Walker, New Society Publishers, Gabriola Island, BC, Canada, 2005

Chain of Command by Seymour M. Hersh, Harper-Collins Publishers, First Harper Perennial Edition, 2005

America Beyond Capitalism by Gar Alperovitz, Wiley Publishers, 2006

Natural Capitalism by Paul Hawken, Amory Lovins, L. Hunter Lovins, Little, Brown and Company, Boston, New York, London, paperback edition, 2000

Restoring the Earth, Visionary Solutions from the Bioneers by Kenny Ausubel, H.J. Kramer Publishers, Tiburon, California, 1997

Magazines & Online Publications:

TomPaine.common sense, May 8, 2007 issue: "Coming Soon to a Toll Booth Near You" by Sam Pizzigati.

What is Enlightenment, Spring/Summer 2003 Issue, article by Jeremy Rifkin (pp. 17-18)

The Mountain Astrologer, Cedar Ridge, CA., Aug/Sept Edition, "Out on the Edge with Sedna" by Brian Trussler , Mercury Direct section, (pp 2-8)

The *Guardian* Unlimited Site (http://www.guardian.co.uk)

Article by Science Editor, Robin McKie, July 19,2003

Article by Jeremy Rifkin, March 1, 2004

Article by Dr. Jeremy Leggett, June 19, 2004

Article in Business Section, Nov. 27, 2006

Buzzflash Site (http://www.buzzflash.com)

Yahoo News, Article January 9, 2005

Platform Press Release (online), March 2, 2007

"Argus" February 11, 2006

The Associated Press (online) February 9, 2007

Znet, February 14, 1005, "The Indian Seed Act and Patent Act – Sowing the Seeds of Dictatorship" by Vandana Shiva

Appendices: Astrological Charts

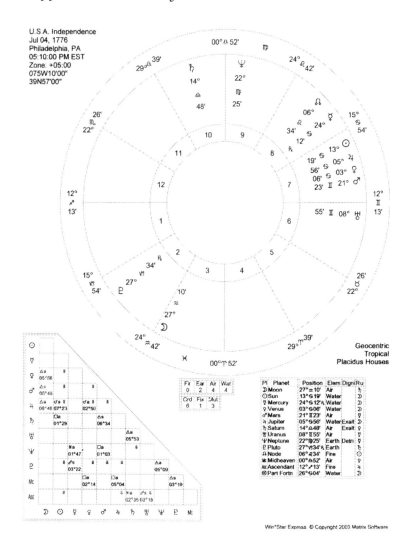

U.S.A. Independence
Jul 04, 1776
Philadelphia, PA
05:10:00 PM EST
Zone: +05:00
075W10'00"
39N57'00"

Geocentric
Tropical
Placidus Houses

Pl	Planet	Position	Elem	Digni	Ru
☽	Moon	27°≈10'	Air		♄
☉	Sun	13°♋19'	Water		☽
☿	Mercury	24°♋12'℞	Water		☽
♀	Venus	03°♋06'	Water		☽
♂	Mars	21°♊23'	Air		☿
♃	Jupiter	05°♋56'	Water	Exalt	☽
♄	Saturn	14°♎48'	Air	Exalt	♀
♅	Uranus	08°♊55'	Air		☿
♆	Neptune	22°♍25'	Earth	Detri	☿
♇	Pluto	27°♑34'℞	Earth		♄
☊	Node	06°♌34'	Fire		☉
⚷	Midheaven	00°♎52'	Air		♀
Asc	Ascendant	12°♐13'	Fire		♃
⊗	Part Fortn	26°♋04'	Water		☽

Fir	Ear	Air	Wat
0	2	4	4

Crd	Fix	Mut
6	1	3

Appendix A: USA Independence, July 4, 1776

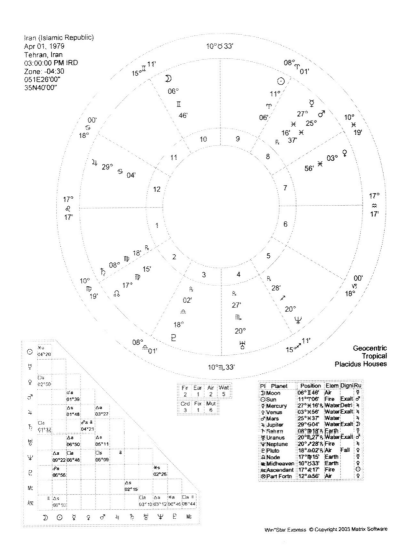

Appendix B: Emergence of the Islamic Republic of Iran, April 1, 1979

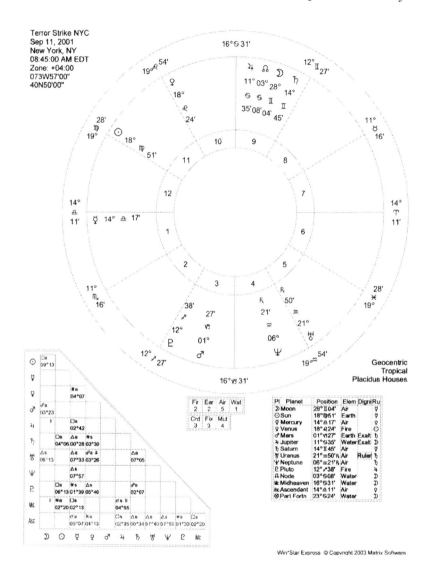

Terror Strike NYC
Sep 11, 2001
New York, NY
08:45:00 AM EDT
Zone: +04:00
073W57'00"
40N50'00"

Geocentric
Tropical
Placidus Houses

Fr	Ear	Air	Wat
2	2	5	1

Crd	Fix	Mut
3	3	4

Pl	Planet	Position	Elem	Digni	Ru
☽	Moon	28°Ⅱ04'	Air		☿
☉	Sun	18°♍51'	Earth		☿
☿	Mercury	14°♎17'	Air		♀
♀	Venus	18°♌24'	Fire		☉
♂	Mars	01°♑27'	Earth	Exalt	♄
♃	Jupiter	11°♋35'	Water	Exalt	☽
♄	Saturn	14°Ⅱ45'	Air		☿
♅	Uranus	21°♒50'℞	Air	Ruler	♄
♆	Neptune	06°♒21'℞	Air		♄
♇	Pluto	12°♐38'	Fire		♃
☊	Node	03°♋08'	Water		☽
⚷	Midheaven	16°♋31'	Water		☽
Asc	Ascendant	14°♎11'	Air		♀
⊗	Part Fortn	23°♋24'	Water		☽

Win*Star Express © Copyright 2003 Matrix Software

Appendix C: Terror Strike, NYC, September 11, 2001

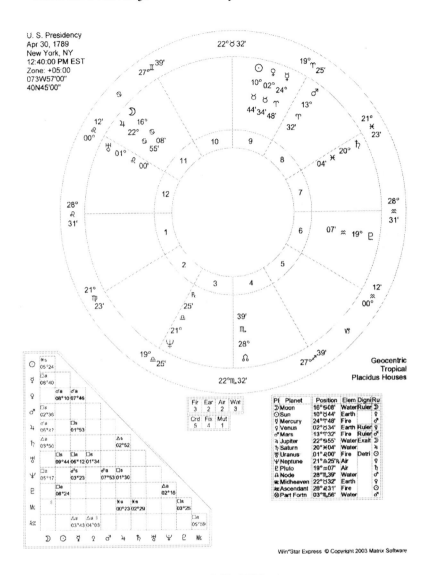

U. S. Presidency
Apr 30, 1789
New York, NY
12:40:00 PM EST
Zone: +05:00
073W57'00"
40N45'00"

Geocentric
Tropical
Placidus Houses

Fir	Ear	Air	Wat
3	2	2	3

Crd	Fix	Mut
5	4	1

Pl	Planet	Position	Elem	Digni	Ru
☽	Moon	16°♋08'	Water	Ruler	☽
☉	Sun	10°♉44'	Earth		♀
☿	Mercury	24°♈48'	Fire		♂
♀	Venus	02°♉34'	Earth	Ruler	♀
♂	Mars	13°♈32'	Fire	Ruler	♂
♃	Jupiter	22°♋55'	Water	Exalt	☽
♄	Saturn	20°♈04'	Water		♃
♅	Uranus	01°♌00'	Fire	Detri	☉
♆	Neptune	21°♎25'℞	Air		♀
♇	Pluto	19°♒07'	Air		♄
☊	Node	28°♏39'	Water		♂
⋆	Midheaven	22°♉32'	Earth		♀
⚵	Ascendant	28°♌31'	Fire		☉
⊕	Part Fortn	03°♏56'	Water		♂

Win*Star Express © Copyright 2003 Matrix Software

Appendix D: U.S. Presidency, April 30, 1789

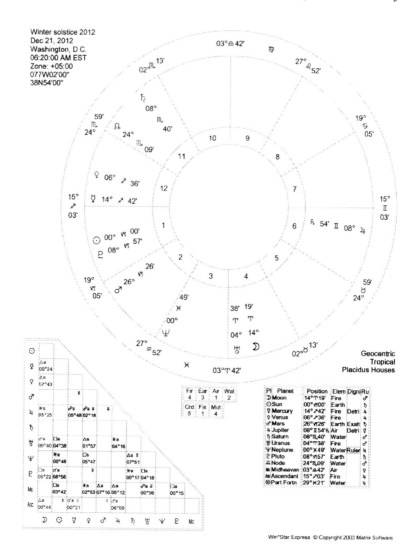

Winter solstice 2012
Dec 21, 2012
Washington, D.C.
06:20:00 AM EST
Zone: +05:00
077W02'00"
38N54'00"

Geocentric
Tropical
Placidus Houses

	Fir	Ear	Air	Wat
	4	3	1	2
	Crd	Fix	Mut	
	5	1	4	

Pl	Planet	Position	Elem	Digni	Ru
☽	Moon	14°♈19'	Fire		♂
☉	Sun	00°♑00'	Earth		♄
☿	Mercury	14°♐42'	Fire	Detri	♃
♀	Venus	06°♐36'	Fire		♃
♂	Mars	26°♑26'	Earth	Exalt	♄
♃	Jupiter	08°♊54'℞	Air	Detri	☿
♄	Saturn	08°♏40'	Water		♂
♅	Uranus	04°♈38'	Fire		♂
♆	Neptune	00°♒49'	Water	Ruler	♃
♇	Pluto	08°♑57'	Earth		♄
☊	Node	24°♏09'	Water		♂
Mc	Midheaven	03°♎42'	Air		♀
As	Ascendant	15°♐03'	Fire		♃
⊗	Part Fortn	29°♓21'	Water		♃

Win*Star Express © Copyright 2003 Matrix Software

Appendix E: Winter Solstice, December 21, 2012

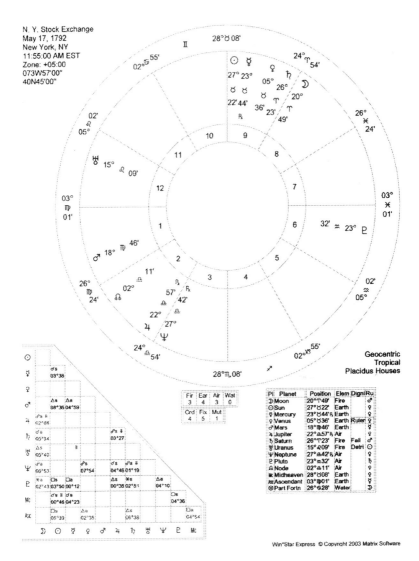

N. Y. Stock Exchange
May 17, 1792
New York, NY
11:55:00 AM EST
Zone: +05:00
073W57'00"
40N45'00"

Geocentric
Tropical
Placidus Houses

Fir	Ear	Air	Wat
3	4	3	0

Crd	Fix	Mut
4	5	1

Pl	Planet	Position	Elem	Digni	Ru
☽	Moon	20°♈49'	Fire		♂
☉	Sun	27°♉22'	Earth		♀
☿	Mercury	23°♉44' ℞	Earth		♀
♀	Venus	05°♉36'	Earth	Ruler	♀
♂	Mars	18°♍46'	Earth		☿
♃	Jupiter	22°♎57' ℞	Air		♀
♄	Saturn	26°♈23'	Fire	Fall	♂
♅	Uranus	15°♌09'	Fire	Detri	☉
♆	Neptune	27°♎42' ℞	Air		♀
♇	Pluto	23°♒32'	Air		♄
☊	Node	02°♎11'	Air		♀
⚷	Midheaven	28°♉08'	Earth		♀
⚹	Ascendant	03°♍01'	Earth		☿
⊕	Part Fortn	26°♑28'	Water		☽

Win*Star Express © Copyright 2003 Matrix Software

Appendix F: Birth of the New York Stock Exchange, May 17, 1792

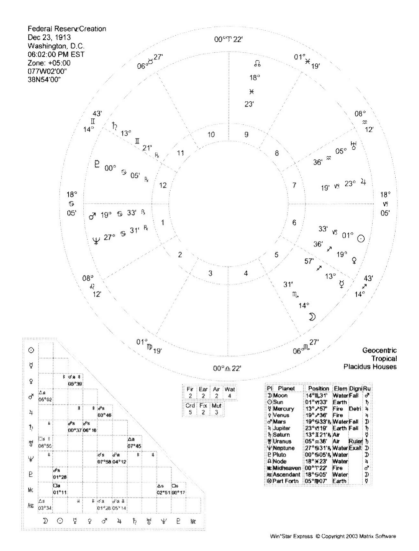

Appendix G: Creation of the Federal Reserve Bank, December 23, 1913

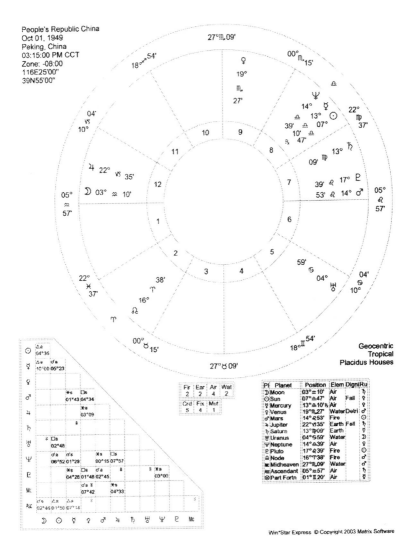

Appendix H: People's Republic of China, October 1, 1949

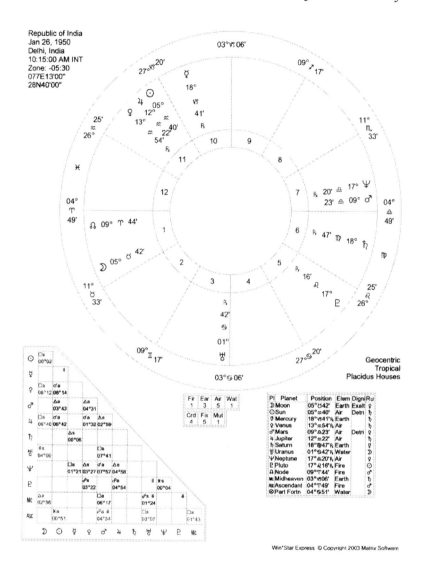

Appendix I: Republic of India, January 26, 1950

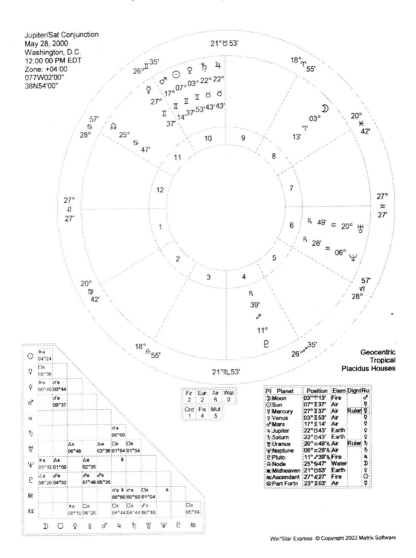

Jupiter/Sat Conjunction
May 28, 2000
Washington, D.C.
12:00 00 PM EDT
Zone: +04:00
077W02'00"
38N54'00"

Geocentric
Tropical
Placidus Houses

Win*Star Express © Copyright 2003 Matrix Software

Appendix J: Jupiter/Saturn Conjunction, May 28, 2000

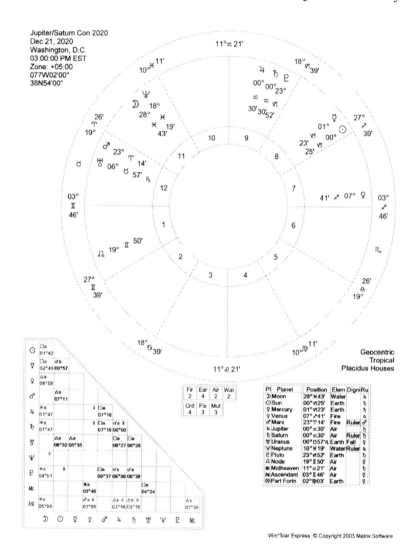

Jupiter/Saturn Con 2020
Dec 21, 2020
Washington, D.C.
03:00:00 PM EST
Zone: +05:00
077W02'00"
38N54'00"

Geocentric
Tropical
Placidus Houses

Fir	Ear	Air	Wat
2	4	2	2
Crd	Fix	Mut	
4	3	3	

Pl	Planet	Position	Elem	Digni	Ru
☽	Moon	28°♓43'	Water		♃
☉	Sun	00°♑25'	Earth		♄
☿	Mercury	01°♑23'	Earth		♄
♀	Venus	07°♐41'	Fire		♃
♂	Mars	23°♈14'	Fire	Ruler	♂
♃	Jupiter	00°♒30'	Air		♄
♄	Saturn	00°♒30'	Air	Ruler	♄
♅	Uranus	06°♉57'℞	Earth	Fall	♀
♆	Neptune	18°♓19'	Water	Ruler	♃
♇	Pluto	23°♑52'	Earth		♄
☊	Node	19°♊50'	Air		☿
Mc	Midheaven	11°♒21'	Air		♄
Asc	Ascendant	03°♊46'	Air		☿
⊕	Part Fortn	02°♍03'	Earth		☿

Appendix K: Jupiter/Saturn Conjunction, December 31, 2020

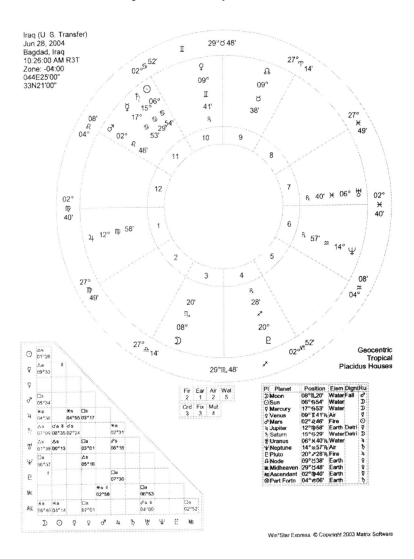

Appendix L: US Transfer of Power to Iraq, June 28, 2004